D1371339

PointMaker™
Devotions for
Youth Ministry

Loveland, Colorado

PointMaker™ Devotions for Youth Ministry

Thanks to the authors and editors of Group's Active Bible Curriculum®, from which this book was compiled.

Credits
Book Acquisitions Editor: Amy Simpson
Compilation Editor: Stephen Parolini
Creative Development Editor: Michael D. Warden
Chief Creative Officer: Joani Schultz
Copy Editor: Candace McMahan
Art Director: Lisa Chandler
Assistant Art Director: Kari K. Monson
Cover Art Director: Lisa Chandler
Cover Designer: Diana Walters
Illustrator: Gary Templin
Production Manager: Gingar Kunkel

Unless otherwise noted, Scriptures quoted from The Youth Bible, New Century Version, copyright © 1991 by Word Publishing, Dallas, Texas 75039. Used by permission.

Library of Congress Cataloging-in-Publication Data
PointMaker devotions for youth ministry.
      p.   cm.
    Includes indexes.
    ISBN 0-7644-2003-8
    1. Teenagers--Prayer-books and devotions--English. 2. Church
group work with teenagers. 3. Christian education of teenagers.
I. Group Publishing.
BV4850.P65 1997
268'.423--dc21

97-13441
CIP

10 9 8 7 6 5 4 3   06 05 04 03 02 01 00 99

Printed in the United States of America.

Visit our Web site: www.grouppublishing.com

Contents

Introduction...6

Learning Experiences

Introduction

"**G**et the point?"

Ever find yourself asking that question of your youth group members, hardly daring to hope that they respond in the affirmative? Ever wonder whether *you* really got the point of a lesson or activity? If so, this book is for you.

Active Learning Works

Learning by doing is what active learning is all about. No more sitting quietly in chairs and listening to a speaker expound theories about God—that's passive learning. Active learning gets kids out of their chairs and into the experience of life. With active learning, kids get to do what they're studying. They *feel* the effects of the principles you teach. They *learn* by experiencing truth firsthand.

Active learning works because it recognizes three basic learning needs kids have and uses them in concert to enable young people to make discoveries on their own and find practical life applications for the truths they believe.

So what are these three basic learning needs?

- Teenagers need action.
- Teenagers need to think.
- Teenagers need to talk.

This collection of forty-five "PointMakers™" is designed to help teenagers explore biblical points by immersing them in experiences that help bring the Bible to life. *PointMaker™ Devotions for Youth Ministry* uses active learning to help group members understand and apply the messages of the devotions.

Active learning happens when students do things that help them understand important principles, messages, and ideas. It's a discovery process that helps kids internalize what they learn. And because none of these experiences has just one point, each of your students can apply the lesson to his or her life in a unique way. This active-learning process helps students understand how the Bible is relevant to their lives.

You can use these PointMakers on their own for brief meetings on particular topics, or you can plug them into your regular meetings—to introduce topics, to help kids explore the topics in detail, or to help kids examine the issues from new perspectives.

No matter how you use this collection of devotions, be sure to dive into the activities with your group members. Don't be a spectator. The PointMakers will be more successful and rewarding to you and your kids if you don't stay on the sidelines.

And be sure to check out the Scripture and topic indexes at the back of the book (pp. 125-127) to guide you to activities that explore a particular topic or Scripture.

If you're looking for activities that kids will remember, look no further. *PointMaker Devotions for Youth Ministry* is your resource.

Get the point?

At Your Service

Purpose:

Kids will learn that being a true leader means serving others.

Supplies:

You'll need a Bible and a variety of other supplies determined by the servant activities chosen for the experience (see "Service Projects" list in margin).

PointMaker

Have kids form pairs. Designate one person in each pair as the "server," the other as the "servee." Select several options from the "Service Projects" list in the margin, or come up with your own options. Direct each servee to choose one of these options for the server to do for him or her within the next fifteen minutes.

When each servee has chosen a service project, have the servers complete these projects for the servees. After all the servees have been served, ask:

● **What was your immediate response when you found out what your role was?** (I was relieved I wasn't a server; I didn't care; I was mad because I wanted someone to give me a back rub.)

● **What was it like to be a servant?** (I felt used; it wasn't as bad as I'd thought it would be; it was fun.)

● **How did it feel to be served?** (It was great; I was a little uncomfortable; I felt stupid.)

● **What surprised you about the experience?** (The servers had as much fun as the servees; I actually envied the servees.)

● **Based on this activity, which person in your pair (the servee or the server) would make a better leader? Explain.** (The servee, because she told the other person what to do; the server because he was doing something to help others.)

● **What lessons can we learn about leadership from this experience?** (You can lead in different ways; to lead, you need to be willing to serve, not just to be served.)

Say: **We usually think of leaders as the people who sit back and call the shots. But God's view of what it takes to be a great leader is closely tied to the experience we just had.**

Ask a student to read aloud John 13:1-20.

Say: **This passage contains a picture of Jesus' model of leadership—**

Service Projects

Use this list of options, some of which may require preparation, or come up with your own ideas:

1. Entertain—Have the servers sing or perform skits for the servees.
2. Do a back and neck massage—Monitor this so no one is rough or inappropriate in any way.
3. Wash someone's hands or feet—Provide a basin, water, soap, and towels.
4. Serve breakfast—Provide juice and pastries. To add flair, include tablecloths and napkins.
5. Tell a bedtime story—Provide children's books for servers to read. Play soft music to complete the mood.

washing his disciples' feet. He set an example of the way he wants us to relate to each other—as servants.

Ask:

● **Do you really believe Jesus' view of leadership is right? Why or why not?** (No, you can't be a servant and have influence; yes, that is how you really change the world; I guess so, but I don't understand it.)

● **How does Jesus' view of leadership compare to the view of leadership you observe at home and at school?** (Leaders usually look for ways to have power over others, not serve them; Jesus' way seems opposite.)

● **How is serving others the same as leading them?** (You're trying to help them by meeting their needs; you help them become what you know they can be.)

● **Based on Jesus' example, how can you be a leader at home, at church or at school?** (I can come early to Bible study and set up the chairs; I can help people with their homework; I can keep my room clean.)

Say: **If you become a leader by gaining power over people, you can change how a person acts outwardly. But if you become a leader by serving people, you can also help change people inwardly, in their hearts. That's the kind of leader Jesus is looking for.**

Balancing the Budget

Purpose:
Kids will experience how difficult it can be to make decisions.

Supplies:
You'll need one photocopy of the "Inapinch Budget Worksheet" (p. 11) for each person, pencils, Bibles, markers, and newsprint.

PointMaker

Form groups of no more than four. Give each group a photocopy of the "Inapinch Budget Worksheet" (p. 11) and a pencil.

Say: **You're members of a fictional country's congress. This country is called Inapinch. Your group has been told to balance the budget by reducing the deficit to zero. In other words, you need to get Inapinch out of a pinch. On your handout is a description of the budget and some possible ways to reduce it. Talk together about workable options, and then decide on a proposal to present to the other groups.**

Allow groups a few minutes to discuss their budgets. Then bring the groups back together. Have groups describe their plans and defend their choices. Then have kids vote on the plan they like best.

Ask:

● **What was difficult about this task?** (Sorting through the options; balancing the good with the bad.)

● **What real-life situations have you been in that made you feel the way you did in this activity?** (Trying to choose what to watch on television; trying to figure out how to spend my money.)

● **How did you arrive at the plan you presented?** (We discussed the options; we compromised.)

● **Did everyone in your group agree on the proposal you submitted? Explain.** (No, we had different opinions on some of the issues; no, we had to compromise; yes, we thought the same way.)

● **How is this exercise like trying to make difficult decisions in real life?** (You need to weigh the options; you can't always do what everyone around you wants; you don't always know enough to make the best choice.)

Form groups of no more than five. Give each group a Bible, a marker, and a sheet of newsprint. Assign one of the following passages to each group: Genesis 39:1-7; Exodus 32:7-10, 19-20; and Matthew 12:9-12. It's OK if more than one group studies the same passage.

Say: **Your passage describes important decisions one or more people were faced with. Read your passage carefully. List on newsprint the options available to the person facing the decision and the potential consequences of each option. For example, one of Joseph's options was to go to bed with Potiphar's wife—but what would the consequences have been? One of Moses' options was to walk away from the Hebrews—but what would the consequences have been? One of Jesus' options was to get angry with the Pharisees—but what would the consequences have been?**

Allow a few minutes for groups to read their passages and write options and consequences on their newsprint. Then bring the groups back together to share their discoveries. After each option is read, have kids stand if they'd choose that option and sit if they wouldn't choose that option.

Have volunteers read the following resolutions to the stories they read earlier: Genesis 39:8-23; Exodus 32:25-29; and Matthew 12:13-14.

Ask:

● **What would you have done in the situation you read about?** (The same thing each person chose; I would've been kinder to the Hebrews than Moses was; I wouldn't have healed on the Sabbath.)

● **Why is it sometimes difficult to find options and weigh the consequences?** (We want all of our consequences to be painless; we like to make decisions quickly; we don't always know the options.)

● **How are the decisions Joseph, Moses, and Jesus faced like the decisions you and I face?** (We all have to make tough decisions; we all have God's help in making decisions; we all feel pressure to make certain decisions.)

Say: **In each of the decisions we read about in the Bible, the person's faith in God played a role in the decision-making process. The key word is "process." Tough decisions shouldn't be made carelessly.**

Inapinch Budget Worksheet

Your job is to reduce the budget deficit. Below is a list of the programs in the budget and how much money is budgeted for each. All budgeted figures for programs are the minimums in order for those programs to work effectively. Most programs could actually use much more money to work well.

The total budget is currently $300 billion. It needs to be $200 billion or less in order to pass. Make the cuts necessary to balance the budget. You may also consider raising the taxes listed below the budget.

Programs in the Budget

Health Care: $50 billion budgeted
Note: Without a strong health-care program, millions of people won't be able to afford doctor bills or hospital costs.

Defense Program: $80 billion budgeted
Note: A weak defense program could mean an attack or takeover attempt by another country.

Education: $30 billion budgeted
Note: Without adequate funding, schools won't be able to hire good teachers, and classrooms will be overcrowded.

Housing: $30 billion budgeted
Note: Even this budgeted amount can't house the millions of people who can't afford housing.

Social Services: $50 billion budgeted
Note: Without sufficient funding, programs to help abused people, addicts, and destitute people will have to be cut.

Space Exploration: $60 billion budgeted
Note: Scientists believe the solution to overpopulation is just around the corner through the space program.

Total: $300 billion

Tax Options

- Raise income taxes 10 percent
- Create "fun" tax (10 percent added to all movie tickets, video games, and sports events tickets)
- Create "education" tax (10 percent added to tuition costs for people who come into the country for education)

Results

Add $10 billion to budget
Add $20 billion to budget

Add $10 billion to budget

Use the chart below to record your final budget proposal:

Health Care: $_____ billion budgeted
Defense Program: $_____ billion budgeted
Education: $_____ billion budgeted
Housing: $_____ billion budgeted
Social Services: $_____ billion budgeted
Space Exploration: $_____ billion budgeted

Total: $_____ (Must be $200 billion or less, unless you use one or more of the tax options.)

Tax Options Used (if any):

Break It Up

Purpose:

Kids will explore what it's like to break up with a boyfriend or girlfriend and discover positive ways to break up.

Supplies:

You'll need Bibles, one photocopy of "Instruction Sheet A" (p. 14) for three out of every four kids, scissors, and one photocopy of "Instruction Sheet B" (p. 15) for one out of every four kids.

PointMaker

Photocopy "Instruction Sheet A" (p. 14), and cut each copy into four sections. Fold each section in half so that kids can't see what's written on other people's papers.

Also make photocopies of "Instruction Sheet B" (p. 15), and cut each one into four sections. Fold these so they look like the others, but keep track of the copies of "Instruction Sheet B."

Have kids form groups of four. (If necessary, form one or two groups of three.)

Say: **I would like each group to brainstorm as many reasons as possible that a guy and girl who like each other should not make a serious commitment to each other to date exclusively. But before you begin, I have a piece of paper for each of you. Please keep it folded until I tell you to look at it.**

Give each student a folded instruction sheet, being sure that one person in each group has one of the sections from "Instruction Sheet B." Remind kids not to look at their own or each other's papers. Don't let students know that some papers are different from others.

Have groups begin their discussions. After one or two minutes, instruct kids to read their papers without letting others see what is written on them. Then have them continue their discussions.

Give the groups enough time to allow the dissenters to try to leave the groups. Then gather all the groups together.

Ask:

● **What happened in your groups?** (We couldn't keep our group together; we ended up fighting.)

● **What was it like when one of your members tried to leave your group?** (I was confused because I didn't know why he wanted to leave; I was upset because she was rude and I was trying to keep the group together.)

● **How was leaving the activity like breaking up with a boyfriend or girlfriend?** (Feelings get hurt; you feel helpless when the other person wants to break up and you don't.)

Say: **It may be your choice to end a relationship, or it may be the** other person's choice. **Either way, you can make breaking up easier—or harder. Let's learn more about various ways to end a relationship.**

Form two groups. Have one group read Luke 6:27-28, 31, and have the other read Galatians 5:15. Ask each group to create and perform a short skit that illustrates the Scripture passage as it relates to ending a dating relationship. Tell kids that the only rule is that everyone must be involved in the acting—either as an actor or as a prop.

Give groups a few minutes to prepare, then have them perform their skits. After the skits, read both Scripture passages aloud to the entire group.

Ask:

● **What would you do if your boyfriend or girlfriend tried to hurt you when your relationship ended?** (I'd be angry; I'd be upset; I'd ignore him.)

● **How can we show love to those who hurt us?** (By not hurting them back; by treating them with respect.)

● **What does it take to end a relationship in a positive, rather than hurtful, way?** (You need to be honest but kind; you need to use positive words.)

Say: **It can be really hard to be loving to those who have hurt us. It's a lot easier to be hateful and bitter. But that bitterness stays with us a long time and becomes a part of the way we act and treat others. Pretty soon we may find out that we haven't hurt only others, but—as Galatians 5:15 says—we have destroyed ourselves as well.**

Instruction Sheet A

Photocopy this page, then cut apart the instructions.

For this activity to work, it is *very* important that your group stay together. Try to be positive and keep your group working together.

For this activity to work, it is *very* important that your group stay together. Try to be positive and keep your group working together.

For this activity to work, it is *very* important that your group stay together. Try to be positive and keep your group working together.

For this activity to work, it is *very* important that your group stay together. Try to be positive and keep your group working together.

Instruction Sheet B

Photocopy this page, then cut apart the instructions.

You're tired of being in this group. Come up with an excuse to leave the group, and say that you are going to join another group.

Begin to argue with everyone, and complain about the group. Tell the others you don't want to be in the group anymore and you don't see any reason to do this stupid activity.

Tell everyone that you don't think you want to be a part of the group anymore. Be very polite, and thank them for helping in the activity. Continue to be polite, but insist on leaving the group.

Be rude to group members, and complain that they never do things the way you want to. Tell them that if they don't start using your answers, you are leaving. Leave even if they *do* use your answers.

Building Bridges

Purpose:

Kids will explore the idea that confidence can build friendships and arrogance can harm friendships.

Supplies:

You'll need Bibles, masking tape, one photocopy of the "Bridge Cards" handout (p. 18) for each group of four people, scissors, one photocopy of the "Boosters and Busters" handout (p. 19) for each person, and pencils.

PointMaker

Lay one long strip of masking tape down each of two sides of the room, about six feet apart. (See the illustration below.)

Have kids form teams of four and face each other, with two kids behind one line and two kids behind the other. (If your group isn't evenly divisible by four, join a group, or assign two people to work as a pair in a team of five.) Give each team a deck of "Bridge Cards" (p. 18) to shuffle and split between them.

Say: **The object of this game is to make a bridge to reach your teammates. The four of you will take turns drawing the cards and doing what they tell you. When you draw a "confidence card," you'll say something that builds up your friendship; then you and your partner will take a step toward your teammates. When you draw an "arrogance card," you'll say something that might harm a friendship; then you and your partner will take a step backward. If your team finally meets in the middle, give your teammates high fives, and sit down.**

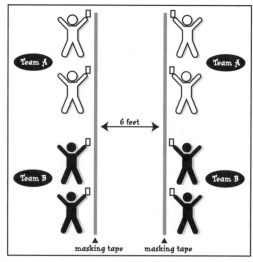

If kids go through their decks without reaching their teammates, have them shuffle the cards and try again. Play until the members of at least half the teams reach one another. If the others aren't able to finish, stop the game anyway. Talk about how arrogance can hurt relationships and become a barrier to communication.

Ask:

● **What were you thinking during this game?** (I was frustrated; I wanted us to get together; just as we made progress, we were split apart.)

● **How is this like friendships in real life?** (Friends drift apart then draw closer; sometimes our words and attitudes drive us apart.)

● **How did you want to respond when someone made an arrogant statement?** (I wanted to act arrogant too; I wanted to laugh.)

● **How did you want to respond when people made confident statements?** (I didn't mind what they said; I was impressed; they still sounded arrogant to me.)

● **Why does having confidence in yourself make it easy to build friendships?** (You already feel good about yourself, so you focus on the other person; you know you have something to offer.)

● **Why do people choose to be arrogant about their accomplishments when they could be quietly confident and affirming to others?** (They may not know the difference; they may be hiding the fact that they're really unsure of themselves.)

Say: **Fortunately, we have more control over how we treat our friends than we had in this game. We can decide to be confident and affirming rather than arrogant. The Bible helps us find the right balance. If we need a confidence booster, we can find it in Scripture. And if our egos need a bit of deflating, Scripture can help us with that, too.**

Give each student a Bible, a photocopy of the "Boosters and Busters" handout (p. 19), and a pencil. Have kids stay in their groups of four for this activity.

Ask kids to give you working definitions of both arrogance and confidence, based on what they've done in class so far.

Say: **Too little confidence and too much arrogance are problems that we find at opposite ends of the self-esteem spectrum. Work in your group to come up with answers to both problems, based on the Scriptures listed on your handout.**

Give groups a few minutes to read the Scriptures and complete their handouts. Then call everyone together, and ask groups to share their completed handouts.

Ask:

● **How do confidence and arrogance affect your relationship with God?** (Confidence draws us closer; arrogance keeps us from knowing God.)

● **How do you think God would describe a confident person?** (Someone who understands what it is to be God's child; someone who believes God is at work in his or her life.)

Say: **Knowing that you're God's child and that he's at work in your life is necessary to the development of healthy self-confidence.**

Bridge Cards

Photocopy this page for each group of four people, and cut apart the cards.

Confidence Give a reason you could be a great friend.	**Confidence** Make a statement about something you'd like to learn from a teammate.	**Confidence** Compliment one of your teammates.	**Confidence** Suggest something the four of you can accomplish together.
Confidence Tell why your teammates are good friends.	**Confidence** Tell one way you could be a better friend to your teammates.	**Confidence** Tell a teammate something you like about him or her.	**Confidence** If you could give your teammates a gift, tell what it would be.
Arrogance Say something that exaggerates your own abilities.	**Arrogance** Explain why none of your partners could be as good a friend as you are.	**Arrogance** Tell why you're a better person than anyone you know.	**Arrogance** Give a reason no one deserves a friend as wonderful as you.
Arrogance Explain why your teammates are lucky to be paired with you.	**Arrogance** Make a statement that exaggerates your own importance.	**Arrogance** Explain why the youth group is better because you're in it.	**Arrogance** Give an example of what people should do for you because you're so great.

Boosters and Busters

Sometimes we need a little boost in our confidence. At other times we may need our arrogance deflated a little. Use these Scripture passages to help you come up with ways to boost confidence and deflate arrogance.

Ephesians 2:8-10
2 Corinthians 3:4-6
2 Corinthians 5:16-17

Confidence Boosters   **Arrogance Busters**

Caring Actions

Purpose:
Kids will learn how they can use their unique abilities to care for others.

Supplies:
You'll need Bibles, newsprint, and markers.

PointMaker

Have kids brainstorm caring actions they can carry out during the meeting. For example, kids might suggest complimenting others, offering hugs, or helping others find Scripture passages. Write kids' suggestions on a sheet of newsprint. Then have kids each choose one action. On "go," have kids perform their caring actions for other people. If you have a small group, you might want to arrange ahead of time to have kids visit other classes to perform the caring actions there as well.

Have kids regroup and form a circle, then ask:

● **What was this experience like for you?** (Uncomfortable; I enjoyed doing something nice for someone.)

● **In what ways did your various caring actions use different abilities?** (Giving compliments required good speaking skills; helping someone find a Scripture required good knowledge of the Bible; giving a hug required freedom to express emotion.)

● **What does this exercise show us about how we can use our unique abilities to help others?** (We don't all have to be great talkers or huggers; each person can offer something different.)

Have each person complete the following sentence: "When I use my abilities to help someone else, I feel…"

Say: **God knows our strengths and weaknesses. And he knows how to help us use our strengths, just as he helped Abraham and Peter.**

Have kids form groups of no more than four. Have someone in each group read aloud Genesis 17:1-8 and Matthew 16:13-19. As kids read, write the following questions on newsprint for groups to discuss:

● What happened to the two men in these passages?

● Why were Abram and Simon given new names?

● What did each new name signify about that person's future?

● How would you feel if God gave you a new name that symbolized how you were to use your abilities?

After groups spend time discussing the questions, say: **Our names identify us but rarely have any deeper meaning. In Bible times, a name often reflected the person's mission or purpose in life.**

Have kids pair up and give their partners new names based on their partners' abilities. Then have kids introduce their partners, using the new names.

The Cheating Box

Purpose:
Kids will learn why it's wrong to cheat.

Supplies:
You'll need to create a "surprise box" before the meeting. Place a snack such as cookies or doughnuts in a plain cardboard box. Also place in the box a sheet of paper with the following written on it:
1. True
2. False
3. False
4. False
5. True

Be sure to close the top so kids can't see in. On the outside of the box, write, "supplies." You'll also need a Bible, paper, pencils, newsprint, and markers.

PointMaker

Set the box you prepared before the lesson on a table in the center of the room. Say: **For this activity, I'll need one volunteer to leave the room with me for a few minutes. While I'm gone, talk with each other about times you've been tempted to cheat. But don't look in the box on the floor. It contains a special surprise and the answers to some quiz questions we'll be asking when we return.**

With your volunteer, leave the room for about three minutes. Explain to the volunteer that you just needed an excuse to leave the room for a few minutes so kids will think about what's in the box. After a few minutes, re-enter the room.

Have kids form a circle around the box. Say: **Before I give you the quiz, I'd like to ask some questions.**

Ask:
● **What was the first thought that came to your mind when I asked you not to look in the box and then left the room?** (I wondered what was in the box; I wondered if we should peek in the box.)

● **How did you feel, knowing there were answers in the box that might help you in class?** (I was confused; I felt uncomfortable.)

● **Would the temptation to cheat have been greater if you had known that the quiz would be graded? Explain.** (Yes, if I'd wanted a good grade, I might've looked in the box; no, I still wouldn't have looked in the box.)

● **How is the temptation to cheat in this activity like the temptation to cheat in school?** (Cheating is too easy in school, just as it would be here; the temptation to cheat at school is much stronger.)

Don't ask kids whether they cheated in this activity. Simply have them discuss the temptation to cheat they may have experienced during this activity and the temptations they feel at school. If you discover that someone cheated or even that the entire class peeked, don't condemn or criticize the kids. Use it as a "teachable moment" to talk about their feelings before and after cheating.

Don't show kids the contents of the box. Set it aside until you need it.

Say: **In Old Testament times, Joseph was tempted to cheat in a different way than you are at school. But his response to the temptation can help you deal with temptations to cheat at school. Listen carefully to the story I'm going to read. In a few minutes, we'll have our quiz to see how well you listened.**

Read aloud Genesis 39:6-12.

Give each person a sheet of paper and a pencil. Have kids number their papers from one to five. Then read the items in the "True or False" box in the margin, and have kids write their answers on their papers.

Open the box you prepared before the meeting, and use the answer sheet you placed there to help kids grade their quizzes. Distribute the special food treats to kids while you go over the answers to the quiz.

Say: **In this story, Joseph had an opportunity to cheat on his boss, but he didn't cheat. In fact, because he didn't give in to the temptation, he was wrongly punished.**

Ask:

● **What might the consequences have been if Joseph had given in to the temptation and had been caught?** (He would've been punished in the same way; he would've been killed.)

● **What might have happened if Joseph had cheated without being caught?** (He'd have felt guilty; he would have been caught eventually.)

True or False

1. Potiphar left Joseph in charge of everything he owned—true or false?

2. Potiphar's wife asked Joseph to run away with her—true or false?

3. Joseph gave in to Potiphar's wife's request—true or false?

4. Potiphar's wife asked Joseph to sleep with her only once—true or false?

5. Joseph fled from Potiphar's wife without his coat—true or false?

Say: **Joseph didn't cheat. And he took definite steps to avoid the temptation to cheat. Let's take a look at the steps he took and think about how they can help us beat the cheating urge.**

Have kids form pairs, then have partners tell each other about times they were tempted to cheat at school. After a few minutes, read aloud each of the following steps Joseph took to avoid the temptation to cheat. After you read each step, write it on a sheet of newsprint, and ask partners to talk about how each step applies to them.

● **Step one: Decide to refuse to cheat** (verse 8).

(Kids might say, "I can choose to always be honest at school.")

● **Step two: Accept full responsibility for what you do** (verse 8).

(Kids might say, "I can't count on someone else to help me overcome the temptation to cheat; I have to live with the consequences of my actions.")

● **Step three: Recognize that God is with you** (verse 9).

(Kids might say, "I can pray and ask for God's help when I'm tempted to cheat.")

● **Step four: Avoid flirting with temptation** (verse 10).

(Kids might say, "I can avoid situations in which I might be tempted to cheat.")

● **Step five: Get away, even if you have to leave something behind** (verse 12).

(Kids might say, "I can walk away from situations in which someone is tempting me to cheat.")

Have kids form a circle and tell what they thought of for each step. Ask volunteers to act out ways to implement each step in tempting situations they can think of. For example, someone might act out a response to a situation in which someone is prompting a friend to give him or her the answers to an upcoming test.

Say: **Joseph's five-step plan helped him avoid cheating. And it can help you overcome the temptation to cheat, too.**

Closed Circles

Purpose:
Kids will discover why it's important to accept others.

Supplies:
You'll need Bibles.

PointMaker

Ask for two or three volunteers. Have the volunteers leave the room. Have the remaining group members form groups of two to six people.

Tell these groups that they are now cliques. Have them form tight circles, facing inward. Have them begin talking within their cliques about a subject of their choice. Instruct the groups to exclude the "outsiders" (your volunteers) from their conversations and physically move as needed to keep them out of their circles.

Bring the outsiders back, and ask them to join any group's conversation. After about two minutes, stop the activity, and have kids form a circle.

Ask the outsiders:

● **What was it like to try to join a group?** (I felt excluded; I couldn't join.)

● **What actions or words did you use to try to join?** (I tried to be polite; I tried to force myself in.)

Ask the other group members:

● **What was it like to keep the outsiders out?** (I didn't like it; I wanted to let them in; it was fun.)

Ask everyone:

● **What aspects of this exercise are like real life?** (People form cliques that others can't join; people try to be friends with people who won't let them.)

Read each of the following sentence-starters, and have at least three people complete each one based on the opening exercise or their real-life experiences with cliques:

● **I tried to join a group of friends by...**
● **We tried to keep someone out of our group by...**
● **When I was excluded from a group's conversation, I felt...**
● **Leaving someone out of our group made me feel...**
● **When I realized I couldn't get into a group, I...**

Ask:

● **How does it feel to be left out?** (Lonely; depressing; it makes me feel as if no one likes me.)

Say: **Being left out isn't much fun, but you're not the only people who have felt excluded from "elite" groups.**

Have kids form four groups, and assign one of the following passages to each group: Mark 2:13-17; Luke 7:36-50; Luke 19:1-10; and John 4:4-10.

Have groups read their passages and then discuss the following questions:

● **How is the situation in your passage like situations in your life?** (I feel like the Samaritan woman sometimes; people in my school exclude others just as the Pharisees did.)

● **By his actions and his words, what has Jesus said about cliques?** (Cliques aren't healthy; cliques separate people; it's better to include people rather than exclude them.)

● **What reassurance has Jesus given to the outsiders in these passages?** (God loves us just the way we are; each person is important; it doesn't matter who your friends are.)

Clues for Survival

Purpose:

Teenagers will discover what it takes to "survive" as Christians in a non-Christian world.

Supplies:

You'll need Bibles; a photocopy of the "Survival Strategy" handout (p. 28) for each person; red, blue, green, and brown markers; pencils; and newsprint.

PointMaker

Before the meeting, photocopy the "Survival Strategy" handout (p. 28), and make a red, blue, green, or brown X at the top of each one. Mark an equal number of handouts with each color, and shuffle the handouts so they'll be distributed randomly.

Give each person a pencil and a handout, and instruct students to leave the handouts face down. Tell kids that each handout represents a passport to one of four places in the world: the Amazon jungle, the Pacific Ocean, the Swiss Alps, or the Sahara Desert.

Say: **Imagine that each of you has taken a vacation by plane to one of the four destinations I mentioned. Ironically, all four planes have crashed. You have ten minutes to locate your fellow passengers and choose from the supply list the five items most needed for survival in your region. Find people with matching X's on their passports, and complete your handout with them. Ready? Go!**

After ten minutes, call groups together, and have them list the supplies they chose and explain their choices. Then ask:

● **What kinds of emotions did you experience as you tried to choose only five items?** (Frustration; anxiety; excitement.)

● **Why was it important to know where you crashed?** (We would have different needs in different places; so we could set our priorities.)

● **How did you decide what to choose?** (We thought ahead to what we might face; we thought of someone who had really crashed.)

● **How is this game like our relationships with God?** (We have to be prepared in the world; we need God to survive; we have to think ahead to what might happen in certain situations.)

● **What do you need to "survive" as a Christian?** (A Bible; strong Christian friends; time with God.)

Say: **You don't become a Christian by accident. People who become Christians decide that a relationship with God is important to them. To make this relationship the best it can be, Christians need certain things**

to "survive" or to stay alive spiritually.

Have kids form three groups, and assign each group one of the following verses: Joshua 1:8; Matthew 14:23; and James 1:27. Give each group a few minutes to look up its verse, decide how the verse relates to a healthy relationship with God, and come up with a two-part skit.

The first part of the skit should demonstrate how *not* obeying the verse affects a person's relationship with God. The second part should show how *obeying* the verse improves a person's relationship with God and shows others what being a Christian really means. For example, the first part could portray a student who claims to be a Christian but ignores the need of a friend who forgot his lunch money. The second part could portray this student sharing his lunch and telling his friend how God motivated him to help.

After each group has performed, have the other groups guess what qualities or practices they were trying to portray. Write the qualities or practices on newsprint, and ask:

● **How did watching these skits affect you?** (I felt kind of guilty because I do the wrong things; it was a good experience because I know our group members usually act appropriately.)

● **How are the characters in your skit like some people you know?** (Some give others a bad impression of Christians; some think being a Christian means just going to church.)

● **From what we have seen through reading our Bibles and watching these skits, how would you summarize God's plan for a strong relationship with him?** (We need to read our Bibles; caring for others is important; prayer is a way to share our lives with God.)

● **Why is it sometimes hard to do these things even though we know they keep us close to God?** (We don't make time; we forget; our friends pull us away from God.)

● **Are you doing anything to make your relationship with God better? If so, what?**

Say: **God wants to have an excellent relationship with each person here, but it takes effort and commitment on our part.**

Survival Strategy

Your plane has crashed. Please check your passport and use this color code to find out where you've crashed: red = the Amazon jungle, blue = the Pacific Ocean, green = the Swiss Alps, and brown = the Sahara Desert.

Once you've located your fellow passengers, look over the supply list, and choose the five most important things you will need to survive in your region.

Supplies: waterproof matches, a tarp, six sleeping bags, a compass, three jugs of water, a battery-operated fan, four candy bars, lipstick, shark repellent, a lantern, an empty ice chest, a life raft, snowshoes, a portable stereo, sunscreen, a kerosene lamp, dehydrated food packs, a rope, two small jackets, an umbrella, a navigation map, a clock, a razor blade, an inner tube, seven flares, an old boat motor, and a radio.

Command Performance

Purpose:

Kids will examine what it means to be humble.

Supplies:

You'll need Bibles, at least one slip of white paper for each person, two slips of red paper, two hats, and a variety of other supplies as dictated by the choices in the opening activity (see below). You'll also need a copy of the "Make Over" handout (p. 31) for each person and pencils.

PointMaker

Put several slips of white paper in two hats. Put one slip of red paper in each hat. Have the guys draw slips of paper out of one hat and the girls out of the other. The guy and girl who draw the red slips of paper are the king and queen. All the other students become serfs. (If no one draws the red slip of paper, have kids keep drawing until someone does.)

Make a big show of announcing the king and queen. Put chairs on a table, and have the serfs help the king and queen up to their royal thrones.

Say: **You serfs are now in the service of the king and queen. You must obey their commands (within reason). Now I'm going to have a royal conference with their majesties, and the rest of you must sit on the floor in silence until we're finished.**

Give the king and queen a suggested list of commands for the serfs. Include ideas such as "Get the juice box in the refrigerator," "Please fetch my royal doughnut from the kitchen," "I require a napkin," "Please dispose of this napkin now," "Do a somersault," and "Sing me a song." Let the activity go on until each serf has served the king and queen in some way. Then have everyone form a circle.

Ask the royalty:

● **What was it like to have special privileges?** (I felt guilty; I enjoyed it.)

Ask the serfs:

● **How did you like being bossed around?** (I didn't mind; it made me angry.)

● **What were your feelings about the king and queen?** (I thought they were cool; I resented them; I wanted their food.)

● **What do you do in real life that reminds you of the role you played here?** (At school I have to do whatever the teachers tell me to do; sometimes my parents make me feel like a serf.)

Say: **Very few of us want to be the underdogs or the people who come in last or the ones who wait on everybody else. It's just human nature to want to be top dog, the best, the fastest, the most powerful. But Jesus showed us that God's nature is quite different from human nature.**

Give each student a "Make Over" handout (p. 31), a Bible, and a pencil. Have kids form three groups, and assign each group one of the make overs on the handout.

Say: **The character you've been given needs a new look. The Scriptures give you clues about how to make the needed changes. When you present your make over to the whole class, everyone in your group should take part. You'll need people to act out or mime your character (both before and after), to narrate, to be the extras, to read Scripture, and to explain what you did in the make over.**

Give groups about five minutes to plan their make overs. Then have them take turns performing for the whole class.

Ask:

● **What were your thoughts about your character before the make over?** (He was pretty obnoxious; she reminded me of people I know.)

● **What was similar about all the make overs?** (All the characters were made more humble.)

Say: **The tricky thing about humility is that it always comes from a position of strength and security. We could take the credit, but we choose to give it to God, knowing that he's our source of security and power. You have to be strong to be humble. That may sound like a contradiction, but it's absolutely true. Jesus gave us a powerful example of how strength and humility work together.**

Make Over

Like all of us, these characters are imperfect people. First read the "Before" column and the Scripture. Then decide what you'd do to make this person reflect the values shown in the verses. Write about the make over in the "After" column.

BEFORE	MAKE OVER MATERIAL	AFTER
Vic lives for the limelight. He wants recognition more than anything else. He has some problems with relationships, but he knows that at this point in his life it's more important to achieve. Later, he figures, there'll be more time for his Christian life and his friendships.	Matthew 5:5	
Joe likes to let everyone know that he and God are close. In fact, he makes a point of slipping it into any conversation on any subject. After all, he says, people need to know who the good guys are. He thinks of himself as the spiritual giant of his high school.	Matthew 6:1-4	
Tessa wants to have a relationship with God, but she's thinking seriously about dropping out of church. She's sick of trying to get along with everyone. She's had it with her family and its rules. She's sick of the group that follows her around at school and church. She's ready to blow off the whole thing and go it alone for a while.	Micah 6:8	

Consequences

Purpose:

Teenagers will explore the consequences of "playing around" sexually.

Supplies:

You'll need photocopies of the "Consequences" box (p. 33), scissors, a box, an egg timer, photocopies of the "Scripture Questions" box in the margin below, and Bibles.

PointMaker

Photocopy the "Consequences" box (p. 33), and cut apart the items. Fold the slips, and place them in a box. Have kids form a circle, and ask:

● **What are risks people take when they play around sexually?**

Have the class mention several, then say: **Today we're going to play a game called Risky Business. I'll set an egg timer and then place it inside a box. We'll pass the box around the circle, never knowing when the timer will go off. In the game, we're going to pretend that all of us have become sexually active. As long as the box is going around and the timer hasn't gone off, we're all playing around sexually with no problems. But when the timer goes off, whoever has the box has to face the consequences of sexual freedom.**

Set the egg timer for ten to thirty seconds, and place it in the box with the "Consequences" slips. Begin passing the box around the circle. Whoever has the box when the timer goes off must draw a slip of paper from the box, read it aloud, and say what he or she would do in the situation described on the slip.

Play several rounds. Each time, set the timer for a different amount of time—from ten to thirty seconds. If you don't have time for all the slips to be drawn, stop the game and read the rest of the consequences aloud.

Ask:

● **How did you feel as the box was passed around?** (Nervous; uncomfortable; anxious.)

● **How is that like the feeling people have when they take chances sexually? Explain.** (It's very similar—you don't know what you're getting into; it's not the same at all—less chance is involved.)

● **How did you feel when you had to choose a**

Scripture Questions

Read aloud Genesis 2:15-17. Then discuss these questions in your group:

● Why does God put limits on our freedom?

● What are the limits of our freedom?

● What happens when we go beyond those limits?

Read aloud Ezekiel 18:26-32. Then discuss these questions in your group:

● Who's responsible and accountable for human behavior?

● When we live outside the boundaries, what happens?

● Why does God allow the consequences of our actions to fall on us?

consequence? (Angry—it was unfair; upset; it didn't bother me.)

● **How did you feel if you never had to suffer one of the consequences?** (Relieved; lucky; happy.)

● **Which consequences of sexual activity scare you the most? Explain.**

Say: **Consequences aren't new. In biblical times, people often dealt with negative consequences of their behavior.**

Form groups of no more than six. Give each group a Bible and one of the two sections of the "Scripture Questions" box (p. 32): Genesis 2:15-17 or Ezekiel 18:26-32. Have each group read its Scripture passage and answer the questions associated with it.

Form two groups—one with all the groups that worked on the Genesis passage and one with all the groups that worked on the Ezekiel passage. Have each group create a brief skit (no more than thirty seconds) to demonstrate the meaning of its passage.

After the groups perform their skits, ask:

● **What are the limits God sets for our sexual behavior?** (Don't have sex before marriage; don't do anything that could be dangerous.)

● **Why do you think God placed these limits on us?** (They're for our own good; God doesn't want us to have any fun.)

● **Why are some consequences irreversible?** (Because they're always in our memories; because we have to live with our mistakes.)

Say: **We live with the consequences of our decisions. But if we've already made mistakes, God is big enough to forgive us and give us a new chance.**

Consequences

Copy this box, then cut apart the items for the Risky Business game.

....

Nothing happens—there are no consequences—yet. How do you feel?

....

Your parents found condoms or birth control pills in your room. They confront you. What do you say?

....

You are (or your girlfriend is) pregnant. What do you say to your parents? your friends?

....

The person you had sex with lost interest in you as soon as you slept with him or her. How do you feel?

....

You have (or your partner has) been using a condom for birth control. The company that manufactures your brand has just issued a recall because the product is defective. What do you do?

....

You have the sexually transmitted disease chlamydia. One of the possibilities is that you'll become sterile. What do you say to your partner? your parents?

....

The person you had sex with is now telling everyone in your school what happened. How do you respond?

....

The person you had sex with has just been diagnosed HIV-positive. How do you feel?

....

Cover Story

Purpose:

Teenagers will discover that the pleasant appearance of alcohol can be deceiving.

Supplies:

You'll need Bibles. You'll also need to prepare three containers. Place a small amount of cooked spaghetti or other noodles in a fancy gift bag. Place torn bits of paper in a plain cardboard box. Then place pieces of candy in a plain, wrinkled paper bag. Be sure to have enough candy for each class member.

PointMaker

Display the three containers, but keep their contents hidden. Ask kids to look at the packaging.
Ask:

● **According to what you see, what might you expect to find in each of these three containers?** (The nice bag will have something good in it; the wrinkled bag is probably filled with trash.)

Ask for three volunteers. Assign each volunteer one of the containers. Have the others in the class call out what they think is in each container.

Have volunteers take turns reaching into their containers (without looking) and pulling out the contents for everyone to see. Then distribute the candy.
Ask:

● **Did anyone guess the exact contents of any of the containers? Why or why not?** (Yes, I thought food would be in the plain bag; no, the contents didn't match the containers.)

Ask the volunteers:

● **What was your reaction when you discovered what was in your container?** (I was surprised; I was grossed out; nothing special.)

Ask everyone:

● **How did you react when you discovered that the contents of a container weren't what you had expected?** (I was surprised; I thought you might try to trick us; I was confused.)

● **Which package best represents the way alcohol is presented in advertising? Explain.** (The fancy bag—ads make alcohol look good; the paper bag—some ads depict alcohol as something to be ashamed of.)

● **How can experimenting with alcohol be like getting a gift bag with wet spaghetti in it?** (It looks great but feels terrible; it's fancy packaging for disgusting stuff.)

● **How is avoiding alcohol like the wrinkled bag with the candy in it?**

(Sometimes an unpopular choice reaps the best rewards; doing the right thing doesn't always look great to others.)

Say: **Sometimes things that look good at first aren't so great once you get into them. Experiences with alcohol are like that for many people.**

Have kids call out negative results of drinking, such as getting sick, getting drunk, and losing control.

Ask:

● **With all the negative results of drinking, why is it still so popular?** (Because everyone drinks; because it's cool; because it makes people seem more mature.)

Say: **Though popular, drinking can have negative side effects. And besides the negative side effects, drinking is illegal for kids your age. The Bible brings up serious questions about the benefits of drinking.**

Form groups of no more than four. Assign each group one of the following Scriptures: Proverbs 20:1; Isaiah 5:11-12; and Romans 14:17-19, 21. It's OK if more than one group studies the same passage. Have each group read its passage, discuss what it says about drinking, then think of a phrase that summarizes what the passage might be saying about drinking. Have groups share their phrases with the other groups.

Ask:

● **How does the advice from Scripture make you feel about drinking?** (I wish it'd just say "don't drink" and make it easier for me to deal with alcohol; I feel good that the Bible warns against drinking.)

● **Would you feel cheated if you followed the Bible's advice about alcohol? Why or why not?** (Yes, I'd miss out on parties; no, I can still have fun without drinking.)

Say: **While it seems difficult to find biblical proof for not drinking at all, the Bible does have a lot to say about the negative effects of drinking.**

Defend Your Stand

Purpose:

Teenagers will experience what it's like to disagree with someone on controversial issues.

Supplies:

You'll need to meet where kids can run around freely. You'll also need Bibles, a tennis ball, two tennis rackets, two empty trash cans, poster board, markers, and scissors.

PointMaker

Quickly set up boundaries for a makeshift soccer field either inside or outside the building in which you regularly meet. Use an overturned trash can as a goal at each end of your "field." Form two teams, and ask each team to select a goalie. Give each goalie a tennis racket.

Say: **We have a field, a tennis ball, two teams, two goalies, and two goals. The rest is up to you. You have three minutes to huddle with your teammates and decide the rules for this game. Questions you should answer include "How can we advance the ball? How can we score? How can we defend our goal? Are we penalized for going out of bounds?" and so on. Everyone on your team must agree to play by the rules you decide on. But don't tell the other team what your rules are.**

Give teams three minutes to devise rules for the game, then have them play for five minutes or so.

After the game, ask:

● **What was it like to play a game with conflicting sets of rules?** (Confusing; frustrating; exciting.)

● **How's that like the feeling you have when you talk to others about an issue such as abortion?** (Similar, it really frustrates me when people don't believe the way I do; different, the people I talk to basically agree with me.)

● **Did you feel pressure to adapt to the other team's rules?** (Yes, I could see they'd win if we didn't change our rules; no, I felt good about our rules.)

● **When do people use conflicting sets of rules in real life?** (At school when we're taking a test; right here in our youth group.)

● **How easy is it for people to agree on the rules or standards of conduct in real life?** (Not too hard—most people agree on what's important; pretty hard—people have different views of what's right and wrong.)

● **How's this game like a situation you've dealt with in real life?** (I've been frustrated by people who seem to follow their own rules; it's hard when people don't agree on what's right.)

Say: **All of us know how frustrating it can be to defend things we know are right. Christians often experience the same feeling with each other because people in the church don't always see eye to eye. The same problem cropped up again and again in the Bible. In Exodus, Moses tried to convince Pharaoh that enslaving the Israelites was wrong. But Pharaoh liked having slaves, so naturally he disagreed.**

Form groups of no more than eight, and assign each group one of the following Scriptures: 1 Corinthians 10:23–11:1 or Acts 15:1-21. Give each group poster board, a marker, scissors, and a Bible.

Say: **Read your Scripture passage, and decide what the controversy it describes was about. Then create a short, living comic strip that tells how and why people today might deal with such a controversy. You will act out the comic strip characters, but you can't speak. You must use your supplies to create "dialogue balloons" that tell the story. For example, if my comic strip character is supposed to say, "You don't know what you're talking about!" I'd have to hold up a poster board "balloon" with those words written on it.**

After a few minutes, have each group present its living comic strip, then ask:

● **According to the Bible, what are key criteria for deciding what's right and wrong in life?** (It should be uplifting to others; it should honor God; it shouldn't be selfish.)

Say: **It is possible to follow these criteria and still disagree with other Christians on some issues. That's because people may have different opinions about what it means to honor God or what it means to be uplifting. But if we focus on these criteria and the wisdom of those who have gone before, we can make good decisions about what's right and wrong in life.**

Did You See It?

Purpose:

Teenagers will examine the influence of television in their lives.

Supplies:

You'll need a Bible, a cassette or CD player or a radio, a photo-copy of the "Give 'Em What They Want" handout (p. 41) for every four students, pencils, and a box full of a variety of props (such as newspapers, old clothes, and other easy-to-find items).

PointMaker

Before this lesson, ask a member of another class to help you. Give this person a cassette or CD player or radio, and ask your helper to enter your classroom and play loud music just as you begin class. Explain that you'll ask your helper a couple of nonsensical questions before he or she should leave the room.

Begin class by saying: **Today we're going to talk about television. As you know, television is one of the most influential forces in our society, mostly because almost everyone watches it.**

Signal the volunteer to enter the room. While the volunteer is in the room (with loud music blaring), ask him or her:

- **Did your dog get the cheese under the umbrella?**
- **Has an orange angelfish flown in yet?**
- **Is there an envelope in your flower bed?**

After the volunteer answers the questions, have him or her leave the room. Then quiz kids on what they remember about the visitor.

Ask:

- **What color were the person's shoes?**
- **What was the title of the song that was playing?**
- **What did I ask the person? How did he (or she) answer each question?**
- **How long was the person in the room?**
- **How was the person holding the cassette (or CD) player (or radio)?**

Add your own questions to the list. Then have the volunteer re-enter the room so kids can see how well they remembered what they saw. Repeat the questions you asked, and see how well kids remember what you asked the volunteer and how he or she answered.

Then ask:

- **How easy was it to remember specifics about our guest? Explain.** (Very easy, I observed the situation carefully; not very easy, I didn't know we'd be quizzed.)
- **How is this like remembering specifics about shows we watch on television?** (Sometimes we remember lots of details; it's easy to forget what we've

just seen.)

Say: **The reason television has so much power is that it can operate on so many levels at once. Just as you couldn't focus on every aspect of our guest, it's difficult to focus on everything that's happening on television. And that could be dangerous if you're receiving negative messages but don't know it because you aren't critically evaluating what you're watching.**

Form groups of no more than four. Say: **Congratulations! Each group now owns a national TV network. Each group represents a different network, and you're all in the midst of a major ratings war. Your challenge is to develop a new show for the annual broadcasters convention that will win in the ratings. I'll give you a handout that lists examples of shows that are currently pulling in high ratings. You'll want to consider those ideas as you prepare your shows.**

Give each group a "Give 'Em What They Want" handout (p. 41) and a pencil. Place a box of miscellaneous items in the center of the room. The box might include such items as old clothes, newspapers, light bulbs, food, and hangers. Almost anything will do.

Say: **Use the handout to begin brainstorming your ratings-winning show. When you've developed your ideas, plan a short excerpt to role play so we can all see what the show is like. I've provided a box of items you can use as props for your show.**

When kids have finished preparing, call the whole group back together, and have each group make its presentation. Declare the winner—the group with the most outrageous idea or the one with the most negative images.

After the presentations, ask:

● **What are your feelings about the winning show?** (I don't like it; we should've won instead.)

● **What elements were included in the shows to make them ratings winners?** (Violence; humor; sexual content.)

● **How did you feel as you tried to create a show that would win the ratings war?** (Anxious; confident; uncomfortable.)

● **How realistic were the people portrayed in the shows? Explain.** (Not very realistic, they seemed too "perfect"; somewhat realistic—they had real-life problems.)

● **Did you feel OK about using negative elements in your show? Why or why not?** (No, I'd rather do a positive show; yes, that's how to improve ratings.)

● **How were the ways groups tried to outdo each other like the ways real networks compete for viewers?** (The networks try to come up with the most outrageous ideas; the networks try to use controversial topics to gain viewers.)

Say: **We're often willing to overlook negative elements or unrealistic portrayals of people when we're being entertained. But if we're not careful, we might feed ourselves too many negative images. Television certainly gives us benefits—the ability to learn about world events as they happen, access to educational and informational shows, inexpensive entertainment—but it can also influence us negatively.**

Have kids sit in a circle. Have each person say one positive thing about television. Tell kids it's OK to repeat someone else's comments. After each person describes a positive trait, tuck your thumbs under your armpits, flap your elbows twice, and squawk like a chicken (or come up with your own silly action and sound). If your group has fewer than ten kids, go around the circle twice.

Afterward, ask:

● **What aspect of this activity stood out the most?** (The strange actions and sounds you made; the list.)

Have volunteers take turns attempting to recite all the benefits of television people called out.

Then ask:

● **How is the way my actions stood out from our discussion like the way negative images sometimes stand out on television?** (The negative stuff is most easily remembered; the negative stuff is always most prominent.)

● **Did my actions enhance or detract from our discussion? Explain.** (They detracted because they were annoying; they enhanced our discussion because they made us laugh.)

Have someone read aloud Romans 12:2.

Ask:

● **What does this verse tell us about the kinds of TV shows we should watch?** (We need to choose carefully what we watch; we need to avoid negative messages.)

● **Based on today's discussion, do you feel a need to change any of your TV-watching habits? If so, how and why?**

Say: **When we watch TV shows that are filled with negative images and messages, we're conforming to the world's standards. But living by God's standards doesn't necessarily mean we have to avoid television. Instead, we should learn to use a filter to evaluate what's worth watching and what's best to avoid.**

Give 'Em What They Want

So, you're a network executive, huh? Well, good luck coming up with the next great TV show. Remember, the following ingredients are currently what the viewing public seems to want: fistfights, murders, special effects, steamy sex scenes, cheating spouses, lying, cruel jokes, stupid parents, bratty kids, and unrealistic characters.

Have fun…you're on your way to the top!

1. Which kind of show will it be? comedy? drama? action-adventure? musical? Remember, you want it to be entertaining.

2. Who are the main characters, and what do they do?

3. What's the setting? city or rural? home or work? big city or small town? rich neighborhood or poor? Describe the setting in detail.

4. Describe a typical episode below. Then plan to act out part of this episode for the other groups. Use any props you need from the box provided.

5. Does the show have a theme song? Describe the song below, or list the title of a real song that best describes your show.

6. If you have time, list the kinds of sponsors you're likely to get for this show. Who will advertise during your prime time slot?

Don't Distract Me

Purpose:

Kids will learn that reaching goals means being committed to overcoming distractions.

Supplies:

You'll need Bibles; newsprint; a basketball; "loud" foods such as potato chips and raw carrots; and any other objects you can use to distract the group members, such as a radio, a squeaky door, or an alarm clock.

PointMaker

Have kids form groups of three. (If necessary, it's OK to form some groups of two or four.) Give each group a sheet of newsprint and a Bible. Say: **Read Proverbs 4:23-27, and talk about what it means to you. Then work together to tear the newsprint into a shape that represents goals you strive for.**

As soon as students start, begin your special mission of distraction. Turn on a radio with loud, annoying music. Dribble a basketball around the room. Talk loudly to another leader about a movie or recent sports event. Eat raw carrots or potato chips. Ignore any annoyed looks or comments from the students, and continue to do everything you can to distract them.

After a few minutes, bring the group together again. Have groups show their torn newsprint and explain what they talked about.

Ask:

● **Were you distracted by any of my actions? If so, why?** (Yes, I couldn't concentrate on the activity because of the noise; no, I'm used to lots of distractions.)

● **What was it like to be distracted while you worked on this activity?** (We were frustrated; we ignored the distractions so they didn't bother us; it was hard to concentrate.)

● **How did my distractions affect your ability to complete the activity to the best of your abilities?** (We couldn't concentrate; some group members were more concerned about the noise than the activity; we didn't get to discuss our ideas much.)

● **In what ways is this activity similar to what you experience at school?** (It's easy to get distracted at school; you don't always have support from the people around you.)

Have someone read Proverbs 4:23-27 aloud. Then ask volunteers to summarize it.

Say: **Reaching any goal, including goals at school, means being committed to overcoming distractions and disappointments so you can stay focused on where you're going.**

Expectations

Purpose:

Kids will explore the difference between caring for others and seeking to please others.

Supplies:

You'll need Bibles and one photocopy of the "Caring Questions" box in the margin below for every four students.

PointMaker

Have kids form groups of no more than four, then have groups stand, facing inward, in a circle. Have each person mime an action or activity that fits each of the following categories:

- My friends' image of me is…
- My parents' image of me is…
- My image of myself is…

Encourage kids to use facial expressions and motions to illustrate the images. Then have kids briefly discuss their actions in their groups.

Ask:

- **What difference (if any) was there in your actions from one category to the next?** (My parents and friends have different images of me; I am just what everyone sees.)

- **What went through your mind as you acted differently for the different categories?** (I wondered why expectations are so different; I felt uncomfortable showing everyone other people's images of me.)

- **How do others' expectations affect how you act?** (Sometimes I act differently so people will accept me; I don't let others' expectations affect me.)

Say: **When we act according to others' expectations, it's often because we want to please them or be accepted. But seeking to please others sometimes keeps us from being ourselves. Instead of striving to please others, we should learn to be ourselves and care for others.**

Jesus dealt with the issue of how to please others. He also dealt with others' expectations.

Have kids form groups of no more than four. Give each group a Bible and a copy of the "Caring Questions" box in the margin. Have groups discuss the questions based on the passages.

Caring Questions

- Read Matthew 16:13-19 and Luke 7:36-50.
- Who did people think Jesus was?
- How do you feel when people describe you as being like someone else?
- Did Jesus change his actions to meet others' expectations? Why or why not?
- Did Jesus try to please others or care for them? Explain.
- How did Jesus care for people in these passages?

Have each group brainstorm two or three differences between pleasing someone and caring about someone. Have each group report these differences to the other groups.

Say: **Jesus knew that his mission was different from what many people thought it should be. But he didn't change his ways to please others. Instead, he used who he was to care about others.**

Family Feuds

Purpose:

Kids will examine why they're sometimes disappointed with their families and explore ways to overcome that disappointment.

Supplies:

You'll need Bibles, enough photocopies of the "Secret Snags" handout (p. 47) for each person to have one section, scissors, one photocopy of the "Family Feuds" handout (p. 48) for each group of two to four people, and pencils.

PointMaker

Before the activity, photocopy the "Secret Snags" handout (p. 47), and cut the sections apart. Also photocopy the "Family Feuds" handout (p. 48).

Have kids form "family groups" of no more than four, and have each person in the group choose one of the following roles: mother, father, or child. Give each family group a photocopy of the "Family Feuds" handout, a pencil, and a Bible.

Say: **I'd like to give each family a chance to discover its knowledge of the Bible. Before we begin, I'll give each person a "secret snag" that will help or hinder your family. Be sure to keep it a secret from everyone in your family, and be sure to do exactly as the paper says.**

Hand out the secret snag slips, and remind students to look only at their own. Then have families begin working on their handouts.

When the families are finished, have each person reveal his or her secret snag to the rest of the family.

Ask:

● **How did your group get along?** (People wouldn't cooperate; someone was picking a fight or ignoring everyone all the time.)

● **How did you react to the way others were behaving?** (I was angry; I felt like quitting.)

● **How are these situations and feelings like problems in your own home?** (I always fight with my brother; my mom tries to get us to work together, but we refuse.)

Answers to "Family Feuds" Handout

● Man kills only brother. (Genesis 4:8-9)

● Morning after wedding, man finds out he has been tricked into marrying the wrong woman. (Genesis 29:21-25)

● Godly priest is found to have evil sons. (1 Samuel 2:11-12).

● Woman raped by her half-brother. (2 Samuel 13:1, 12-14)

● King marries 700 women. Problems sure to follow. (1 Kings 11:1-3)

● Man claims his beautiful wife is his sister. (Genesis 12:11-13)

● Queen kills her entire family to preserve her place on the throne. One baby secretly saved. (2 Kings 11:1-3)

● Brother sells his inheritance for a quick meal. (Genesis 25:29-34)

● Letter to church offers advice to kids and their parents. (Ephesians 6:14)

● Widow poses as a prostitute in order to become pregnant by her father-in-law. (Genesis 38:15-19)

● Two sisters who want children get their father drunk so he will sleep with them. (Genesis 19:30-36)

● **What secret snags reminded you of yourself?**

● **What other things cause disappointment in families?** (Broken promises; divorce; alcoholism; workaholism.)

● **How could you have avoided the problems in this activity?** (We could have just tried to get along; we could have tried to listen to one another.)

● **What secret snags hindered the family relationships in the Bible stories you read?**

● **How can you work together in your real family to avoid disappointing experiences like this one?** (We can talk about our feelings; we can be patient with each other.)

Say: **There are all kinds of secret snags that keep us from getting along with family members. But when we learn to work together and overcome these obstacles, we can overcome disappointments in our families.**

Secret Snags

Photocopy and cut apart these instructions as indicated.

You are too cool for this activity. Ignore everyone in your family.	Make everyone happy. Agree with the others even if they're wrong.
Do your best to help your family cooperate.	Argue with all the others even if you think they may be right.
Make fun of every answer given by the person sitting to your right.	Hog the Bible, and don't let anyone help you look up the verses.
This is such a boring activity. Be sure everyone knows how bored you are.	Be as helpful as possible so your family will do its best.
Turn your chair around, and face the opposite direction. You can participate; just don't look at anyone.	Try to cheat by sneaking over to the other teams and glancing at their answers.
Cooperate, and try to get everyone in your family to work together.	Brag about how easy this is and how anyone who doesn't understand isn't as smart as you are.
Keep changing the subject. Talk about the weather, your clothes, sports, television—anything but the activity.	Try to get everyone to work together to help your family come in first!
Complain about how unfair this activity is.	Encourage each family member to do his or her best.
Don't agree with anything said by the person sitting to your left.	Threaten to leave the group if everyone doesn't work together and win.
Listen and smile, but don't offer any help in getting this done.	Keep poking the people sitting next to you with your elbows.

Family Feuds

Find the Scripture reference that matches each Bible headline.

Man kills only brother.

Morning after wedding, man finds out he has been tricked into marrying the wrong woman.

Godly priest is found to have evil sons.

Woman raped by her half-brother.

King marries 700 women.
Problems sure to follow.

Man claims his beautiful wife is his sister.

Queen kills her entire family to preserve her place on the throne. One baby secretly saved.

Brother sells his inheritance for a quick meal.

Letter to church offers advice to kids and their parents.

Widow poses as a prostitute in order to become pregnant by her father-in-law.

Two sisters who want children get their father drunk so he will sleep with them.

Genesis 25:29-34; 1 Samuel 2:11-12; Genesis 38:15-19; Genesis 19:30-36; Ephesians 6:1-4; Genesis 12:11-13; 2 Samuel 13:1, 12-14; 1 Kings 11:1-3; Genesis 29:21-25; Genesis 4:8-9; 2 Kings 11:1-3

Far From God

Purpose:

Kids will discover that God draws them near to him despite the times they let him down.

Supplies:

You'll need Bibles, paper, and pencils.

PointMaker

Form a circle so that each person's right shoulder is toward the center. Stand in the center of the circle, and instruct teenagers to move in as close as possible.

Say: **When a person first becomes a Christian, he or she usually feels really close to God. Let's imagine that this ring you've formed represents God. Each of you is as close as you can get. I'm going to read some situations and instructions. Follow the instructions as they apply to you. Be honest.**

Read these instructions slowly:

● **If you argued with anyone this week, take a step away from the center.**

● **If you seriously thought about cheating on a homework assignment or test this week, take a step away from the center.**

● **If you read your Bible every day this week, take one step closer to the center.**

● **If you talked about someone behind his or her back this week, take a step away from the center.**

● **If you prayed at least three times this week, take a step closer to the center.**

● **If you talked about your faith with a non-Christian friend this week, move one step closer to the center.**

● **If you didn't, take a step away from the center.**

● **If you were honest on all the preceding questions, take a step toward the center.**

Ask kids to notice how far from the center they are standing, then ask:

● **What did it feel like to admit you had done something that moved you away from God?** (I felt guilty; I was embarrassed.)

● **How did you feel when you knew you'd done something to bring you closer to God? Explain.** (Glad; I took a bigger step toward the center.)

● **How is this experience like your relationship with God in real life?** (I move closer or further away by my actions; he always waits for us to come back, just as the center of the circle never moved.)

● **What are other things that cause you to feel far from God?** (My doubts about him; when I pretend I'm not a Christian so people will like me.)

Have kids form two groups. Provide each group with a Bible, paper, and a pencil. Ask one group to look up Mark 14:29-31, 66-72, and ask the other group to look up John 21:15-19.

Tell each group to read its passage and prepare a news report telling what happened. Give the groups these reporting rules:

1. The information must be accurate.

2. Everyone must be involved in the report in some way.

Allow time for the groups to prepare. Then have the group that studied Mark present its report. After the report, ask:

● **How do you think Peter felt when he realized what he'd done?** (Stupid; ashamed.)

● **Do you think it was harder for Peter to follow Christ after he made this blunder? Why or why not?** (Yes, because he felt ashamed; it wouldn't matter, because he knew God would forgive him.)

● **Have you ever felt the way Peter did? If so, when?**

● **How did you respond to God in that situation?**

Say: **In Peter's story, the way Peter dealt with God wasn't nearly as important as the way God dealt with Peter. Let's have our second report now.**

After the second report, applaud both groups' efforts. Then ask:

● **How did Jesus respond to Peter's sin?** (He forgave Peter; he loved him anyway.)

● **What can we learn about God's ways in our own lives when we think we've disappointed him?** (God will always forgive us if we ask; God loves us no matter what we do.)

Give kids a few moments to pray and interact with God about times they've disappointed him. Allow plenty of time for kids to work through their feelings silently, then close with prayers asking for forgiveness.

Say: **Peter went on to be a great leader of the church. The difficulties in his relationship with God made him a stronger Christian. The disappointments we face in our relationships with God can ultimately make us into stronger Christians, too.**

_____

Find or Fail

Purpose:

Teenagers will examine the feelings they have when they fail.

Supplies:

You'll need Bibles, a food prize (such as doughnuts or candy), and scissors. For every six people you'll also need one photocopy of the "Successful Failure" handout (p. 53), one bowl or small box, and a die.

PointMaker

Before the meeting, photocopy the "Successful Failure" handout (p. 53), cut it into strips, and put the strips in a bowl or a small box. You'll need one set of strips for every six students.

Have kids form teams of no more than four.

Say: **This is a scavenger hunt. I'll name four items, and the first team to return with everything wins. There's a three-minute time limit, so if you haven't found everything by then, return with what you have. You can stick together, but your chances of winning will be better if each person chooses an item and you separate.**

Show students the prize you'll award the winning team.

Name four items you've chosen that could be found on the church grounds, such as a church bulletin, a paper clip, the pastor's autograph, a crayon, or a paper towel. Select items that will take kids a few minutes to locate. Remind kids to return within three minutes, then send kids on their hunt.

> ### Hint
> If a team has fewer than four members, at least one member will need to find more than one item.

When everyone returns, determine which team gathered all the items first, and award the winning team its prize. If no team gathered all the items, award the prize to the team that returned first with the most items.

Ask:

● **Did you feel pressure during this game? If so, why?** (I didn't want to let my team down; I knew my teammates wanted the prize; I didn't know where to find my item.)

● **What kind of pressure did you feel during this game?** (Pressure to hurry; pressure to win; pressure to find my item.)

● **How did you feel if you couldn't find your item? Explain.** (I felt I was letting my team down; frustrated; as if I'd failed.)

● **How is the pressure to win this game like real life?** (I can't do everything I'm supposed to; I have to do things to make others happy; failing to complete a job is disappointing.)

Say: **The feelings accompanying failure are usually negative, and some-times the fear of failing is just as bad as actually failing. But failure can lead to positive changes. Let's examine the story of a guy who failed in a big way and see how it affected his life.**

Have kids form groups of no more than six. Give each group a set of "Successful Failure" strips and a die. Each group will also need a Bible.

Say: **Read Matthew 26:33-35, 69-75 and John 21:15-19 together. Determine how Peter failed and what Jesus did about it.**

Allow several minutes for reading and discussion.

Say: **Assign each person in your group a number from one to six. Roll the die. If your number appears, take a paper strip from the bowl, and answer the question on it. If a person has already had two turns to share and his or her number is rolled, he or she may select someone else to take a turn.**

After a few minutes, have students regroup.

Ask:

● **Do you ever feel the way Peter did? If so, when?** (When I say things I can't live up to; when I make mistakes; when I let someone down.)

● **What encourages you after failure?** (Being forgiven; people telling me they understand; trying again and succeeding.)

Say: **After Jesus' talk with Peter, Peter went on to become a great church leader. He was faithful even until his death.**

Successful Failure

Photocopy this page, and cut apart the strips. You'll need one photocopy for every six students.

What do you think Peter's failure was? Tell about a time in your life you could identify with him.

Tell about a time you were overconfident and then failed miserably. How did you feel?

Talk about someone you admire in spite of his or her faults.

Talk about how you react to failure. Why do you think Peter might have reacted as he did?

Tell about a time you let someone down and he or she forgave you. How did you feel?

Talk about how you feel when someone lets you down. How easy is it for you to forgive that person?

Tell about a time you failed in a relationship and the person still cared about you. How is that like God's love for us when we fail?

Talk about how your faith helps you handle fear of failure.

Tell about a time you didn't try something new because you were afraid of failing.

Tell about a time you tried something difficult and succeeded.

Talk about the person you would most hate to let down.

Tell about a time you did everything wrong but things worked out anyway. How is this like Peter's story?

What did Peter learn from his failure?

How do you think Peter felt when he heard the rooster crow? Can you think of a time you felt that way?

Follow the Crowd

Purpose:

Kids will explore the pressure society puts on people to conform.

Supplies:

You'll need a Bible and masking tape.

PointMaker

Say: **I'm going to call out two activities. You must choose one and do it. The activity the majority does is the socially acceptable one. Those choosing the socially inappropriate thing will immediately be out and must sit down.**

As soon as you read the choices, each student must choose one and do it. Have kids help you determine which activity is more popular, and have those in the minority sit down. Continue to play the game as time allows. Use the following activities, or make up your own:

● **Bark like a dog, or hoot like an owl.**
● **Give high fives to others, or take off your shoes.**
● **Scratch your head, or rub your stomach.**
● **Hop on one foot, or spin in place.**
● **Recite your favorite Bible verse, or sing the national anthem.**
● **Shake hands with someone, or wave to a friend across the room.**
● **Pretend to comb your hair, or pretend to brush your teeth.**

Have everyone sit down, then ask:

● **How did you feel as you tried to figure out what the socially acceptable thing would be?** (I felt awkward; I was nervous; I didn't want to be embarrassed.)

● **How did you feel when you wanted to do one thing but it wasn't socially acceptable?** (I felt stupid doing my own thing; determined to do what I wanted to do; resigned to joining in.)

● **How is this game like everyday life?** (People aren't accepted when they're different; we're pressured to be like others; we're afraid of seeming different.)

Say: **Everyone experiences social pressure to some degree. Unfortunately, what society expects and what God expects can often conflict.**

Place a strip of masking tape on the floor across the middle of the room. Have students form groups of no more than four.

Have a volunteer read Romans 12:2 aloud. Allow a moment for groups to discuss each of the following questions before sharing their answers with the entire group, then proceed to the next question.

Ask:

● **Who do you think "the people of this world" are?** (People who don't believe in Jesus; people who aren't doing what God wants; anyone who lives in the world.)

● **Why doesn't God want us to change to be like them?** (They're not following God; we should try to be like God instead.)

● **How do people of this world—that is, society—pressure you to change?** (By saying I'm worthless if I'm different; by making fun of those who do their own thing.)

Say: **I'm going to read situations in which you might feel pressured by society. After I read each situation, I'll ask two questions.**

Have kids stand on one side of the tape as you read the situations and ask the questions one at a time. When one student shares an answer, have him or her step across the tape. Anyone who agrees with that answer and has nothing more to add may also step across the tape. Ask those who haven't yet stepped across the tape to share their answers, once again having all those who agree step across the tape. When all unique answers have been given and all the kids have stepped across, read the next question or situation and repeat the process.

Situation one: **A girl in your class is a typical nerd. Her hair looks greasy, her clothes don't fit, and she has an annoying laugh. She also has no friends.**

Ask:

● **If you're conforming to society, how will you treat this girl?** (Ignore her; make fun of her; leave her out of activities.)

> # Hint
>
> If everyone steps across after the first person answers, repeat the question to encourage more discussion.

● **If you're living to please God, how will you treat her?** (Talk to her before class; invite her to church; ask her to sit with me at lunch.)

Situation two: **The most popular kids at school party every Friday night. This includes heavy drinking, and drugs are available too. They invite you to join them.**

Ask:

● **What pressures make this invitation appealing?** (Wanting to be popular; wanting people to like me; wanting to be accepted by popular kids.)

● **What response would be pleasing to God?** (Decline the invitation and invite the kids to a church activity; go to the party but don't drink.)

Situation three: **Your fourth-grade brother loves to hang out with you, but your friends think he's a jerk. His school is having a special skate-night this Friday, and he asks you to go with him. Your friends want you to go to the movies with them.**

Ask:

● **What pressures would you feel in this situation?** (Wanting to be with my friends; wanting to not look like a jerk; wanting to make my brother happy.)

● **What would God want you to do?** (Go with my brother; invite my brother to the movies; do something else with my brother.)

Have everyone sit down, then ask:

● **What's difficult about the biblical responses?** (Others wouldn't understand; I'd feel uncomfortable; I might be expected to do more than I feel ready to.)

● **Why does God want you to be different?** (He wants others to know I'm a Christian; God doesn't want me to sin; God knows what's best for me; God wants me to help others and not to worry about my popularity.)

Say: **When we try to be like everyone else, we smash ourselves into a tiny mold. God has a bigger plan for us, outside of society's mold.**

Follow the Leader

Purpose:

Kids will discover what it takes to be a good leader.

Supplies:

You'll need Bibles and three photocopies of the "Leadership" handout (p. 58).

PointMaker

During the week before the meeting, ask one of your more creative kids to be the leader in the classic children's game Follow the Leader. Encourage your leader to plan fun places to lead the group, such as in one door of the church van and out the other. Also encourage fun activities, such as making faces at the babies in the nursery. Be sure to specify any areas or actions that are off-limits, but give the leader enough freedom to make the game interesting.

Then, during the meeting, instruct the rest of your students to follow the leader wherever he or she goes and to do whatever he or she does.

After the game, ask:

● **What was fun and what wasn't fun about this game? Explain.** (It was great getting to go outside; I felt stupid skipping along the sidewalk; I didn't like doing crazy things in front of my friends.)

● **What key element makes this game fun to play?** (Who your leader is; whether or not you're in the mood to play.)

● **How was playing this game like following leaders in real life? How was it different? Explain.** (Leaders sometimes make you do things you wouldn't otherwise do; they can help you feel like you're a part of something.)

● **What are some positive and negative experiences you have had as a result of following others in real life?** (I got in trouble last year because of one friend; I had a teacher who really helped me grow as a student and as a person; I don't think I really follow anybody.)

● **How are followers influenced by the leaders they follow?** (Followers usually act like their leaders; followers end up just like their leaders.)

Say: **In real life the leaders we follow determine the kind of leaders we'll become. That means we need to be careful about who we follow.**

Have kids form three groups, and give each group a Bible and a copy of the "Leadership" handout (p. 58). (If your group is very large, form more groups, but make sure the total number of groups is a multiple of three.) Assign each group one of the Scripture passages listed on the "Leadership" handout. Have kids read the passage together and report on it. Instruct each group to give its report in the form of a cheer that begins with "If you want to be a leader, first you have to..."

Walk among the groups, offering assistance. Helpful hints are also listed in each section of the handout.

When groups are ready, have them present their cheers. Then have kids turn to partners and respond to the following questions:

- **Who would you like to be more like?**
- **What do you admire about the person you chose?**
- **How would following him or her make you a better person? a better leader?**
- **What are some specific ways you can follow in this person's footsteps?**

When pairs have finished, ask everyone:

- **Why do you think we're talking so much about following in a lesson about becoming a leader?** (Because you become like those you follow; because you have to learn to follow before you can lead.)
- **What's the first step in becoming the kind of leader God wants you to be?** (Choosing to follow the kind of leader God wants; asking God to show you who to follow.)

Say: **We're all going to be leaders of some kind. To become the best leaders we can, we must choose to follow the best leaders we can. In your group, decide how you will commit to following the person you named (or someone else you've chosen), and tell your group what you've decided. Be specific in saying how you will follow your leader.**

Pause as students share, then say: **As a way to solidify your commitment, join hands with your group members and pray that you'll all become the kind of leaders God is looking for.**

Leadership

Deuteronomy 31:1-8

Hint: What type of relationship do you think Joshua and Moses had? How did that affect Joshua as a leader?

Luke 9:23; 14:28-33

Hint: What does it cost to follow Jesus Christ in the twentieth century? What kind of leader will that make you?

1 Corinthians 11:1

Hint: Read 1 Corinthians 3:1-10. What did the Corinthians need to start focusing on in a leader? What type of person are we supposed to follow?

The Fruits of Love

Purpose:
Kids will discover why it's important to save sex for marriage.

Supplies:
You'll need two pieces of fruit (such as apples or firm peaches) for every two to four people and Bibles.

PointMaker

In a room with an uncarpeted, hard floor, have kids form groups of no more than four. If your room is carpeted, place newspapers over the carpeting. Give each group two pieces of fruit (apples or firm peaches work best). Have each group stand, form a circle, and place one piece of fruit in the center of the circle. Have someone in each group hold the other piece of fruit.

Say: **In your group, talk about the pros and cons of having sex before marriage. Also talk about how the media portray sex. As you talk, toss one piece of fruit around your circle. Whenever you hear a pro for having sex before marriage, drop the fruit, then pick it up and begin again. You'll have four minutes to discuss your feelings about the subject.**

On "go," have groups begin discussing and tossing the fruit. Walk among the groups and help keep the conversations going. After four minutes, call time. Have kids remain in their circles and sit down. Then have them pass around the two pieces of fruit for everyone to inspect.

Ask:
● **How does the piece of fruit you've been tossing around look?** (Ugly; bruised; gross.)

● **By comparison, how does the fruit that remained in the center of the circle look?** (Much better; more appetizing.)

● **Which piece of fruit would you rather eat? Which would you rather be? Explain.**

● **How is someone who has sex before marriage like the bruised fruit?** (He or she might feel used; he or she might have emotional bruises just as the fruit has bruises.)

Say: **The potential negative aspects of sex before marriage aren't always as obvious as the bruises on the fruit. Sometimes they're well-hidden and may not appear until after that person is married. God created sex as a beautiful expression of two people's love for each other. And he created the marriage relationship as the context for sex.**

Ask:
● **How do you think God feels when his followers choose to save sex until marriage?** (Happy; thrilled; pleased.)

Say: **God smiles on our decisions to follow his Word. And when we make mistakes, he has the power to renew us so we can begin again to do his will.**

Ask:

● **Why should God care if we have sex or not?** (Because God loves us; it's not God's business; God doesn't want us to have fun; God doesn't want us to be hurt.)

Say: **The Christian faith has always placed sex in the context of the marriage relationship. We're going to look at some Scripture passages to help us understand why.**

Form groups of no more than six. Give each group a Bible and assign one of the following passages: Matthew 22:34-40; Romans 6:12-20; and Ephesians 5:1-20. Make sure all three passages are assigned.

Have each group read its passage and prepare to answer the following questions:

● **What concern is expressed in this passage?**

● **Why is it important?**

● **How does it relate to having or not having sex?**

Have each group present the message of its passage to the other groups as if students were talking to their own teenage sons and daughters.

Say: **God cares about us and wants what's best for us. God wants us to have healthy, supportive relationships—and to save sex for marriage.**

Grades and Efforts

Purpose:
Kids will discover the value of learning, apart from getting good grades.

Supplies:
You'll need one photocopy of the "Graded Activity" handout (p. 63) for every four people, one photocopy of the "Best Effort" handout (p. 63) for every four people, pencils, newsprint, masking tape, markers, and Bibles.

PointMaker

Have kids form pairs. Give half of the pairs photocopies of the "Graded Activity" handout (p. 63) and the other pairs photocopies of the "Best Effort" handout (p. 63). Tell pairs not to show their handouts to other groups.

Place a supply of pencils, newsprint, masking tape, and markers in the center of the room.

Say: **You'll have seven minutes to complete the activity described on your handout. After time is up, I'll evaluate how well you followed your instructions.**

On "go," have pairs begin their tasks. Kids may discuss their activities with their partners but not with other pairs.

After seven minutes, call time, and have pairs who were given the "Graded Activity" handouts stand on one side of the room and pairs who were given the "Best Effort" handouts stand on the other side of the room. Grade the trophies created by the "Graded Activity" pairs. Give grades of B's and C's at random, but don't give any A's, D's, or F's. Then congratulate each of the "Best Effort" pairs on their effort.

Have kids form a circle and place their trophies in the center of the circle.

Ask the "Graded Activity" pairs:

● **What went through your mind when you read your instructions?** (I felt pressured; I was nervous; I felt challenged.)

● **What were your reactions to the grades you received for your work?** (I was pleased; I was unhappy; I was upset.)

● **How is this like the way you or your friends feel about schoolwork?** (Sometimes I feel pressure to get good grades; I usually feel bad about my grades.)

Ask the "Best Effort" pairs:

● **What went through your mind when you read your instructions?** (I felt confident; I felt challenged.)

● **How did you feel when you received praise for your effort?** (Good; happy.)

● **How is this like the way you feel when something goes right at**

school? (Sometimes I feel good about what I do in class; sometimes I feel confident in my abilities.)

Ask everyone:

● **What motivated the different pairs to complete the project?** (Getting a good grade; satisfaction; the desire to do well.)

● **What's more important at school—getting the best grades or learning something? Explain.** (Getting the best grades, because you can get better jobs that way; learning, because you can use your knowledge to do good things.)

Say: **While teachers sometimes focus on the results of your efforts, God is more interested in your actual efforts.**

Let's learn more about God's perspective by taking a look at the "grades" Joseph received in his life from the people around him—and from God.

Copy "Joseph's Report Card" from the box in the margin onto a sheet of newsprint.

Have a volunteer read aloud each of the passages listed on "Joseph's Report Card."

Then have kids imagine they're the people in Joseph's life—his brothers, employer, and friend—and ask them to evaluate what happened in Joseph's life in each situation. Have the class discuss and agree upon a grade to give Joseph for each subject, based on the outcome of the situation. For example, in Genesis 37:5-11, Joseph's brothers might give him a C or a D for talking about his dreams.

After the grades have been chosen, have kids write them on "Joseph's Report Card," then say: **Now that we have grades for each situation, I'd like to give Joseph his final grade: an A.** Mark an A at the top of the card, and circle it.

Ask:

● **Why do you think I gave Joseph an A as his final grade?** Students may think you made a mistake or you graded unfairly because you like Joseph. After kids suggest answers, explain that Joseph earned an A because God's grade is the one that ultimately matters. Joseph did his best and was faithful to God.

Then ask:

● **What pleased God about Joseph's life?** (He was faithful; he did his best.)

● **How can you please God with your schoolwork?** (Do my best; be faithful in doing my homework.)

Say: **Joseph didn't have a perfect life filled with straight A's, but he did work hard to serve God and do his best. He discovered that learning was more important than getting good grades. We, too, can discover the value of learning apart from getting good grades.**

> ## Hint
>
> If you think the "Best Effort" pairs didn't put much effort into their projects, ask them why they didn't seem to try. Discuss the difficulty teachers could have if they graded only effort. Discuss how a combination of results and effort go into teachers' grades of students' work.

Joseph's Report Card

Subject	Passage	Grade
Family Living	Genesis 37:5-11	
Employer Relationships	Genesis 39:16-20	
Friendships	Genesis 40:23	
Faithfulness to God	Genesis 45:5-8	

Graded Activity

Your assignment is to build and decorate a paper trophy, using newsprint, pencils, markers, and masking tape. The trophy can represent a reward for any accomplishments you and your partner have felt good about in the past month.

After time is up, your finished trophy will be graded on originality, quality, and design. You may receive any grade between A and F, so make sure your finished product is great.

Best Effort

At school, you're probably used to being graded for your work. But during this activity, the only grade you'll get will be based on your effort. The finished product is less important than the effort you put into it, so do your best.

Your assignment is to build and decorate a paper trophy, using newsprint, pencils, markers, and masking tape. The trophy can represent a reward for any accomplishments you and your partner have felt good about in the past month.

Have fun!

Guidance

Purpose:

Teenagers will explore how to discover and follow God's will.

Supplies:

You'll need four photocopies of the "Guidance" puzzle handout
(p. 66), scissors, Bibles, paper, pencils, newsprint, and a marker.

PointMaker

Before class, make four photocopies of the "Guidance" puzzle handout (p. 66), and cut apart the puzzle pieces from three of the handouts.

Have kids form three teams, and give each team a stack of puzzle pieces from one handout. Say: **When the pieces are arranged properly, they'll reveal something God gives to every Christian. Let's see which team can put the puzzle together first.**

Students will almost certainly not be able to solve the puzzle. After a few moments of frustration, give one of the teams a copy of the handout with the directions on it. Whisper to the team members that when they have solved the puzzle, they may verbally tell one other team the secret, *if* that team asks them.

After several minutes, ask:

● **What were your feelings during this exercise?** (I was frustrated—I couldn't figure out how to put the puzzle together; I was excited—it was a fun challenge.)

● **What went through your mind when I gave your team the directions?** (I was relieved; I was sorry for the teams that didn't have them.)

● **What was it like to be left in the dark while other people knew the key? Explain.** (I was angry; I felt left out.)

● **How is this activity like trying to figure out God's will?** (It's hard to figure it out on your own; it's easier to figure out God's will when you have the Bible or help from someone else to guide you.)

● **How can you apply this to your life today?** (I can read the Bible more to help me determine God's will; I can listen to other Christians who have been in similar situations before.)

Say: **Life can be a lot like this puzzle. But God has given us instructions through the Bible and the Holy Spirit so that we can better understand the "big picture."**

Form groups of four, and assign each group one of these two passages: 2 Timothy 3:16-17 and James 1:5-6. Give each group a Bible, a sheet of paper, and a pencil. Tell each group to discover and write down what its assigned passage says about finding God's will.

When groups are finished, ask them to share their answers with the rest of the class. Write groups' responses on newsprint.

Ask:

● **How do these methods relate to the puzzle activity we did earlier?** (Reading the Bible is like looking at the directions; listening to the counsel of others is like being told by the other group how to make it work.)

● **How does the Holy Spirit help us understand God's will?** (The Spirit speaks to us through the Bible or through other people; the Spirit speaks to us in our hearts to tell us which way is right.)

● **What should you do when the Bible, other people, and what you feel in your heart don't agree?** (Look to the Bible first because it's never wrong; follow where you think God is leading you even if someone disagrees.)

Say: **Several ways are provided for us to find God's will for our lives. Working together as a whole, these ways almost always make a clear path for us to follow and help us know we are in God's will.**

Guidance

Make four photocopies of this page. Cut out the black shapes, and give one set of them to each of the three teams as puzzle pieces. Keep the extra photocopy to give to one team for the directions.

The Harsh Taskmaster

Purpose:

Kids will experience one aspect of independence.

Supplies:

Before the lesson you'll need to mess up your meeting room. Toss dirty clothes around the room, scatter dirty dishes around, set up an ironing board, and mess up the furniture to give the appearance of a messy apartment. Whatever you do, make sure you can mess it up again in the same way. When kids arrive, tell them to ignore the mess. Kids may wonder what's going on and ask questions about the mess. If they do, tell them to imagine that the room is a college student's apartment, and you'll explain why it's messy later in the lesson. You'll also need newsprint, tape, a marker, and a Bible.

PointMaker

Form two teams, and identify them as Team 1 and Team 2. Say: **We're going to have a contest between these two teams. Team members, pretend that you're roommates and you've just gotten home from work. Look around—this is your apartment. Unfortunately, you have a party starting at your place in a few minutes, and you aren't ready for it. Each team will have two minutes to straighten up this place before guests arrive. Then I'll rate each team's preparedness on a scale of one to ten.**

We'll start with Team 1. You can do anything you want to get this room ready in two minutes, but keep everything in this room.

On "go," start timing the first team. While they're cleaning up, try some tricks such as "calling" them on the phone, sending in a "neighbor" from the other team to borrow something, or having a "guest" arrive early. When the two minutes are up, rate the preparedness of the room on a scale of one to ten. Don't be too generous with your ranking. Identify specifics that aren't perfect, and deduct points for those items.

Mess up the room again, and have Team 2 attempt to clean the room. Once again, interrupt the team's efforts with "visitors" and "guests" arriving early.

After scoring Team 2, have kids discuss the following questions:

● **What emotions did you experience during this activity?** (Frustration; anxiety; none.)

● **How is this like the feeling people might have when they're living on**

their own? (It's similar because they probably feel rushed; it's similar because they probably feel frustrated about living with roommates.)

● **How is this activity like independent living? How is it different? Explain.** (It's similar because you can't depend on your mom to clean up after you anymore; it's different because most people are more responsible than that.)

● **What new pressures did you feel in this activity that you don't feel now while you're living at home?** (The pressure to keep the room clean; the pressure to keep things organized.)

● **What are some pressures adults have that kids living at home don't have?** (Paying bills; working full time; taking care of family members.)

Have everyone work together to straighten up the room.

Tape two large sheets of newsprint to the wall. Write the heading "When I was a child…" on one newsprint sheet and "But when I became an adult…" on the other.

Have a volunteer read aloud 1 Corinthians 13:9-12. Then have each person write a phrase or draw a picture on each piece of newsprint that represents a major advantage or disadvantage of that time of life. For example, on the "When I was a child…" newsprint someone might write, "I didn't have many responsibilities" or "I couldn't do much on my own." On the "But when I became an adult…" newsprint someone might write, "I can do whatever I want" or "I have too many bills to pay."

After everyone has finished, ask kids to explain their pictures or phrases.

Say: **There is no perfect time for becoming independent. No matter when you go out on your own, you'll probably discover many things you wish you'd already learned. But the key to successfully developing your independence is in putting away childish things and learning to be responsible.**

———————————————————————

Just Another Bad Movie

Purpose:
Kids will experience what it feels like when a teenager leaves home.

Supplies:
You'll need one photocopy of the "Script Notes" handout (p. 71) for each person, pipe cleaners, and a Bible.

PointMaker

Have kids form pairs. Have partners decide who will be the "parent" and who will be the "teenager." Say: **I'm sure most of you have seen a movie with a plot like this: Some freak event happens, and an adult trades places with a child. They spend the whole movie trying to get back into their original bodies, and they always succeed. Well, today I'd like you to pretend you're a character in one of those movies.**

Here's the scenario: It's a week after graduation, and your family is working out exactly what's going to happen to you now. One night while you're sleeping, a lightning bolt strikes your house. You wake up in the wrong body! Since you can't do anything about it, you decide to go on with your planning.

To make things easier for you, I'm providing each of you with special script notes. Use these as you work out what you're going to do. After you understand how to play your role, work with your partner to finish your planning. Be sure to stay in character.

After making sure everyone knows what to do, distribute a photocopy of the "Script Notes" handout (p. 71) to each person. Give pairs a few minutes to role play, planning what the teenager will do in the future.

Then bring the group back together and ask:

● **How comfortable were you with the role you played? Explain.** (Very, because I understand the other person's position; not very, I don't play roles well.)

● **What was it like playing the part of the parent?** (Uncomfortable; frustrating; sad.)

● **What emotions did you experience, playing the part of the teenager?** (Confidence; worry; sadness.)

● **What does this role-play reveal about what families experience when teenagers leave home?** (Parents are really sad; teenagers are excited about becoming independent.)

● **How much thought has your family put into your leaving home, and how much have you talked about it?**

Have kids get back in their pairs. Give each person a pipe cleaner. As you read aloud Genesis 12:1-5, have students imagine that they are Abram's parents and are saying goodbye to him. Encourage students to shape their pipe cleaners into symbols of gifts they would give to Abram if they were his parents.

Ask:

● **How is this story similar to what happens when people leave home today? How is it different? Explain.** (It's the same—someday you have to leave everything; it's different—he was so old.)

● **How do you think Abram's family felt as they said goodbye?** (Sad; relieved, they'd probably been trying to get rid of him for years.)

● **How is this like the way parents and kids react when they say goodbye after graduation?** (It's similar; it's harder when your kids are younger.)

Read aloud Luke 15:11-32.

Ask:

● **Why did the prodigal son rehearse a speech to make to his father?** (He was afraid he wouldn't have the right words; he really wanted his father to accept him.)

● **How easy or difficult is it to think of things to say when you've hurt a parent? Explain.** (It's difficult because I feel so bad; it's easy because my parents are understanding.)

Say: **One of the most difficult things parents must do is say goodbye to a son or daughter. By opening the lines of communication and realizing that your parents are facing a difficult situation, you can help make the inevitable separation easier for everyone.**

Have partners trade pipe-cleaner goodbye gifts and encourage each other to always take the first step in communication.

Script Notes

Parent

Begin your role-play by reminding your teenager of how much you know about independence and leaving home—remember, you've been there. Then use the following attitudes and ideas to convince your teenager that college, work, or staying at home (choose one) is the best thing to do.

It's not as if you don't trust your child, but there are a lot of dangers in making the transition into adult life. You'd like to protect him or her if you can.

Your teenager probably doesn't understand what you're talking about when you tell him or her how hard money is to come by, how lonely it is to be away from home, how important it is to work hard, how dangerous it is to have the wrong friends, and how important it is to have some kind of plan for life.

The tough part of your job is to listen to whatever your teenager says and find some way to keep him or her from making mistakes without appearing to be trying to run your teenager's life. Maybe you're a little afraid of losing your child, too.

It's hard for you to stop giving advice, and you keep reminding your teenager of how much you love him or her.

Teenager

Begin your role-play by reminding your parent of your age and ability to take care of yourself. Then use the following attitudes and ideas to convince your parent that what you plan to do after high school is a good idea.

Face it—it's an exciting time to be alive! You have so much ahead of you and so much to do, it's hard to decide exactly what you want to do. Maybe you don't even want to go to college just now. You could travel the world, join the military, get a regular job, or maybe just hang around for a while until you're ready to commit yourself to something for the rest of your life.

You don't see what all the fuss is about. Leaving home is an exciting adventure, and you can pretty much take care of yourself. It'll feel good to get out from under parental influence. Maybe you'll stay away for a while, at least until you get homesick. The important part is to get going and get started with your life—to do what you want to do.

You have to admit, though, that you really worry about things sometimes. It's nice to have a place where you feel cared for, especially in an emergency. You hope that your parents will be understanding enough to help you get started but also to leave the door open in case you need comfort or guidance.

Liars Club

Purpose:

Kids will explore the negative consequences of lying.

Supplies:

You'll need a photocopy of the "Liars Club Application" handout (p. 74) for each person, pencils, tape, newsprint, markers, and Bibles.

PointMaker

Give each person a copy of the "Liars Club Application" handout (p. 74) and a pencil. Have kids complete the handout. Then have kids line up according to the time they went to bed last night—from earliest to latest. Beginning with the person on the "latest" end of the line, have kids each read aloud the items on their handouts.

After kids have read their handouts, have them tape the handouts to the wall. Have kids place a mark in the Truth or Lie column for each item listed on each handout—based on whether they believe that person was telling the truth or lying.

Have kids take turns telling which items on their handouts were lies and which were true. Have kids total the number of incorrect guesses on their sheets to see how well they were able to fool everyone else. Award the person whose handout has the most incorrect guesses the honorary title of Liars Club President.

Ask:

● **What went through your mind as you wrote your lies?** (I thought about real lies I'd told in the past; I didn't feel comfortable with it; it was fun to make up stuff.)

● **How was this activity like constructing lies to tell friends, teachers, or parents? How was it different?** (It's a challenge to make up believable lies; it's difficult to make up lies; it's easy to lie to people.)

● **What were you thinking as you told your lies (and truths) to the rest of the group?** (I felt nervous; I wondered if they could see through my lies.)

● **How is that like the way you feel when you tell people lies in real life?** (I worry about what they're thinking; I feel nervous.)

Say: **In this activity, lying seemed fairly harmless. That's because we all knew the goal of the activity. But in real life, lying can be destructive.**

Have kids form groups of no more than five. Give each group a sheet of newsprint and a marker. Assign each group one of the following Scripture passages:

● Genesis 3:1-6 (The serpent lied to Eve; evil entered the world.)

● Genesis 27:18-41 (Jacob lied to Isaac; Jacob received Esau's blessing; Esau vowed to kill Jacob.)

● Genesis 39:7-20 (Potiphar's wife lied about Joseph; Joseph was thrown into jail.)

● Luke 22:54-62 (Peter denied Jesus; Peter grieved.)

Have groups read their passages and list on their newsprint the lies people told and the consequences of each lie. Have kids form a circle, and ask someone from each group to describe his or her group's findings.

Ask:

● **What can we learn from these stories?** (Lying isn't good; lying separates us from God; lying may seem positive but usually has negative consequences.)

● **What are the long-term effects of lying?** (People are hurt; people become bitter; relationships are broken.)

Have someone read aloud Proverbs 17:20. Then ask:

● **What does this verse say about lying?** (When you lie, it'll come back to you; lying often has negative results.)

Say: **God wants us to be truthful with one another. Lies are destructive, but truth—though sometimes painful—can heal. And when we're honest with others, we show we are responsible in what we say and do.**

Liars Club Application

How good are you at lying? Let's find out.

In each of the six spaces below, describe something you've done or something unique about yourself. But here's the trick: At least one of the things you write must be a lie. If you want to, you may write two lies or three or even six. Just be sure you write at least one lie.

Other kids will be trying to guess whether your descriptions are true, so make your lies convincing. Some things you can describe about yourself might include where you were born, trips you've taken, awards you've received, and people you've met. If you've done some unbelievable things, list them—you might fool somebody.

Name: Truth   Lie

1.

2.

3.

4.

5.

6.

Total incorrect guesses:

Life-and-Death Matters

Purpose:
Kids will experience what it feels like to express their opinions about controversial issues.

Supplies:
You'll need newsprint, tape, markers, and Bibles.

PointMaker

Tape two sheets of newsprint—one labeled "Abortion" and the other labeled "Mercy Killing"—to two opposite walls. Have kids form teams of three, and give each team a marker and a Bible. (If necessary, it's OK to have a team of two or four.) Ask each team to select a "runner."

Say: **I'm going to call out some Scripture references one at a time. Your team's task is to find each Scripture passage and decide whether it says anything about abortion or mercy killing. If you think it does, send your runner to the appropriate piece of newsprint to write down what it says. The first team to write an insight on either of the newsprint sheets wins three points. And every team that writes an insight wins a point.**

If you don't think the Scripture passage addresses either of these two issues, write that on the newsprint and be prepared to explain why. Then we'll all vote on your answer. If the majority agrees with you, your team will receive three points.

Call out these Scripture references:
- **Genesis 1:27**
- **Exodus 20:13**
- **Exodus 21:22-24**
- **Psalm 8:4-8**
- **Psalm 82:3-4**
- **Psalm 139:13-16**
- **Matthew 25:40**
- **Acts 10:34**
- **Ephesians 6:9**

After the last round, declare a winning team, and ask:
- **Was it hard to determine the Bible's position on these issues?** (No, I think it is pretty clear; yes, nothing is really black and white.)
- **Do you agree with the Bible's perspective on these issues? Explain.**

(Yes, the Bible's answers make sense; no, the Bible is too strict.)

● **What kind of pressure did you feel to write insights on your newsprint?** (I wanted our team to win; we had limited time to react.)

● **How is the pressure you felt to act in this activity like the pressure people feel to respond to controversial issues such as abortion and mercy killing?** (People are anxious to solve each crisis in their own way; people are pressured to make decisions before they have time to think about the answers.)

● **Has this experience changed your opinion on the issues of abortion and mercy killing? Explain.**

Say: **In this activity, you had to move quickly to win points. People who have strong feelings about a particular topic often feel that they should act right away on that issue. But it's important to study what the Bible says about an issue before making snap decisions about it.**

———————————————————

Living in a Material World

Purpose:
Kids will examine what success means in worldly and biblical terms.

Supplies:
You'll need card games such as Go Fish, Crazy Eights, or War; one photocopy of "The Material World" role sheet (p. 79) for each person; paper; pencils; Bibles; newsprint; and markers.

PointMaker

Have kids form groups of six or fewer. Give each group a card game.

Before kids start playing, ask one person from each group to serve as an observer. Take the observers aside, and tell them it's their responsibility to watch each person in the group during the game. Show them "The Material World" role sheets (p. 79) so they know what they're watching for. Give them paper and pencils, and tell them to take notes on how the players act and how their actions affect the game. Tell the observers not to say anything to the group.

Next, hand out "The Material World" role sheets to the rest of the participants, and tell them not to let anyone see what their roles are. Don't tell kids that they all have the same role. Instruct players to remember that it's important to stay in their roles at all times while playing the game.

Allow the games to be played for a few minutes. Watch for any deteriorating behavior. Then ask observers to report what happened and who did what to whom in their groups.

After the reports, ask:

● **How did you react during the game?** (I got angry; I was frustrated; I had fun thinking up ways to cheat.)

● **How did you respond to the other players?** (I didn't care what they were doing; I didn't want to trust them.)

● **How is seeking the world's definition of success sometimes like the way you played this game?** (It's "every man for himself"; you have to look out for number one; winning is everything.)

● **How does this method of achieving success affect people?** (It makes them insensitive to others; it makes them distrustful of others.)

Say: **You've just experienced what it means to live in a materialistic world. It's a part of our nature called sin. Our natural desire is to get** ahead and to be successful—no matter what it costs. The message to be the best and to have the most is not only all around us, but it's also in us—and we all struggle with it at times.

Let's explore this further. Finish this sentence: "The area in which I always want to be number one is... "

You might give a few examples—such as "at school," "with brothers and sisters," or "in sports"—to spark kids' ideas. Have several group members complete the sentence.

After kids respond, have them form groups of four or five. Give each group a Bible, a sheet of newsprint, and a marker. Instruct each group to divide its newsprint into two columns. Tell kids to draw in the first column symbols of society's definition of success.

When they've finished, have students in each group read Luke 1:46-55 aloud together. Then have each group draw in the second column symbols of Mary's definition of success.

After they've finished drawing their pictures, have each group appoint a representative to explain the symbols on both sides of the newsprint.

After the explanations, ask:

● **How do these symbols reflect the two views of success?**

● **Who (or what) gets left out of the picture in society's view of success?** (Friends; relatives; anything that interferes.)

● **What were some of the appealing and not-so-appealing aspects of Mary's success?** (An embarrassing pregnancy; the risk of losing her husband; being part of God's redemptive plan.)

Give each group another sheet of newsprint. Tell kids to read John 13:5-17 and draw symbols of Jesus' idea of success.

When they're finished, have groups talk about their symbols.

Then ask:

● **How do you think the disciples felt when Jesus washed their feet?** (Stunned; surprised; embarrassed.)

● **On what levels did Jesus put servants and masters?** (They're equals; they're co-workers.)

● **How would you have reacted if you'd been there when Jesus was washing feet?** (I would have stopped him; I might have asked him to wash mine; I would have asked him to explain what he was doing.)

● **How can you incorporate Mary's and Jesus' views of success into your own?**

Say: **The world's view of success is constantly being shoved down our throats. But Jesus' radical view of success has nothing to do with riding the crest of the latest "gotta buy this" wave. Instead, success means serving. When we follow Jesus' example of servanthood, we'll discover the true meaning of success in our own lives.**

The Material World

Role Sheet

You must win this game. For you there are no rules other than that you must win. You may cheat, lie, or do anything else in your power to win. That's all that's important. Don't let anyone else know what your role is.

Lotsa-Luck Lotto

Purpose:

Teenagers will explore the dangers of pursuing wealth as a life-long goal.

Supplies:

You'll need plenty of photocopies of the "Lotsa-Luck Lotto" handout (p. 82), scissors, pencils, dice, a photocopy of the "Ruler Words" handout (p. 83) for each person, and Bibles.

PointMaker

Give each student twenty $100 bills from the photocopies of the "Lotsa-Luck Lotto" handout (p. 82). Have kids form groups of no more than six. Give each group a pencil and two photocopies of the betting guide from the "Lotsa-Luck Lotto" handout.

Say: **We're going to play Lotsa-Luck Lotto. The object of this game is to end up with the most money. Beginning with the person in your group whose birthday is closest to today, you'll each choose a number between two and twelve. Then write your name on the betting guide next to the number you chose for that round. Place the amount of money you want to bet in the "pool" space on the betting guide. Each person must choose a different number and must bet at least $100 but no more than $300. Each player must bet at least the same amount as the first player.**

For each turn, I'll roll the dice and call out the winning number. If your cash is on that number, you win all the money in the pool for that round. If no one picks the right number, the money continues to accumulate in the pool until someone wins a round.

Tell kids to place their bets. Then roll the dice, and call out the winning number. Have kids take turns being the first person to choose a number. Play ten rounds (or more, if you give each team additional copies of the betting guide). Kids may start to get into this game after a few rounds as they try to win the most money.

After the game, have kids call out their total cash amounts. Reward the person with the most money by having all the other kids give him or her their play money.

Ask:

● **How did people's fortunes change throughout the game?** (People were winning for a while then started losing every time; they didn't change much.)

● **Would you continue playing the game if you could? Why or why not?** (Yes, I 'd like to win more money; no, I've won enough; no, I've lost too much already.)

● **How did you feel when you won a round?** (Great; stunned; happy.)

● **How is that like the way people feel when they receive a lot of money or get a raise?** (It's a great feeling to get a lot of money; people who make a lot of money don't get excited about it after a while.)

● **In what ways did thoughts of winning control your bets?** (I found myself betting everything I could to win; I tried to think of ways to cheat.)

● **How is this like the way people act in real life?** (People do whatever they can to get money; some people throw money away in lotteries, hoping to win big; some people cheat to make money.)

Say: **In this game, the prospect of winning a lot of money kept people playing. But as in life, some people are bound to lose more than they win if they make wealth a primary goal. Let's take a look at what Jesus had to say about the importance of money and wealth.**

Give each person a photocopy of the "Ruler Words" handout (p. 83), a Bible, and a pencil. Have kids follow the directions and write the appropriate words in the spaces provided.

When students have finished, say: **A long time ago, Jesus discovered someone who loved money just as people do today. We've all heard the story, but this time we'll add a personal twist: You're the rich young ruler!**

Read "The Rich Young Ruler" (in the margin) aloud to your students, pausing when you come to each blank space. Each time you pause, ask a teenager to read what he or she wrote for that numbered item. The result will be a humorous, yet personal story about the rich young ruler. If time allows, read the story again, and ask different students to respond until everyone has provided at least one word.

Ask:

● **How are you like the rich young ruler? How are you different?** (I like to buy things; I enjoy money, but I don't often let it control me.)

● **If Jesus asked you to sell everything, would you do it to follow him? Why or why not?** (Yes, I'd trust him to provide; I don't know, it would be difficult to actually do.)

Say: **If money becomes more important than our relationship with God, we've got problems. Following Jesus should come before following a goal to become rich.**

The Rich Young Ruler

A __(1)__ came to Jesus and asked, "Teacher, what good thing must I do to have life forever?"

Jesus answered, "Why do you ask me about what is good? Only God is good. But if you want to have life forever, obey the commands."

__(2)__ asked, "Which commands?"

Jesus answered, " 'You must not __(3)__ anyone. You must not be guilty of __(4)__, you must not __(5)__, you must not __(6)__ about your neighbor, honor your __(7)__ and __(8)__, and love your neighbor __(9)__ as you love yourself.' "

__(2)__ said, "I have obeyed all these things. What else do I need to do?"

Jesus answered, "If you want to be perfect, then go and sell __(10)__ and give the money to __(11)__. If you do this, you will have treasure in heaven. Then come and follow me."

But when __(2)__ heard this, he (she) left sorrowfully, because he (she) was rich.

Then Jesus said to his followers, "I tell you the truth, it will be hard for a rich person to enter the kingdom of heaven. Yes, I tell you that it is easier for a __(12)__ to go through the __(13)__ than for __(14)__ to enter the kingdom of God" (Matthew 19:16-24).

Lotsa-Luck Lotto

Betting Guide

Dice Roll	Round 1 Names:	Round 2 Names:	Round 3 Names:	Round 4 Names:	Round 5 Names:
2					
3					
4					
5					
6					
7					
8					
9					
10					
11					
12					

Pool

Ruler Words

Think of a word to fit each category below. In a few minutes, we'll read a new version of the story of the rich young ruler found in Matthew.

1. A person's occupation: _____

2. Your name: _____

3. Something you've done that was wrong: _____

4. Another thing you've done that was wrong: _____

5. Something other people do that's wrong: _____

6. Another thing other people do that's wrong: _____

7. Someone you care for: _____

8. Someone else you care for: _____

9. A neighbor's name: _____

10. The most expensive item you own: _____

11. The name of your church: _____

12. A very large item: _____

13. A very small item with a hole in it: _____

14. The name of a rich person: _____

Masterpiece Theater

Purpose:
Kids will think about how God sees them.

Supplies:
Before the meeting, prepare a prop box. Include items such as paper, pencils, index cards, cloth, a needle, wire, a hammer, nails, wood, a radio, a calculator, and other items to represent kids' various interests and skills. You'll also need one photocopy of the "Talking to the Artist" handout (p. 86) for each person, Bibles, and pencils.

PointMaker

Bring out the prop box you've prepared. (If you have a large group, form two smaller groups and provide two prop boxes.) Briefly display and identify each item in the box. Explain that kids will have the opportunity to be "on stage" and express something unique about themselves to the rest of the group.

Say: **You'll have twenty seconds to demonstrate a talent, skill, or interest you have, using any of the objects in this box as a prop. You might demonstrate a skill by actually doing it and giving some "how to" steps. Or you can simply tell what you're interested in and why and something about your experience with it. You'll have one minute for planning and preparation, starting right now.**

Let kids look through the items in the prop box. Call time after one minute, and ask the person with the most recent birthday to begin. After each person finishes, have kids applaud, then brainstorm for no more than twenty seconds a list of ways this skill or talent could be used in the future. For example, kids might tell someone who demonstrates writing that he or she could be a great novelist someday. Or kids might tell someone who describes an interest in music that he or she could be a disc jockey someday. Then repeat the process with the person who has the next most recent birthday.

When everyone has finished, have the students take a bow. Then have kids form a large circle.

Ask:

● **How does it feel to try to express something important about yourself in a short amount of time?** (Frustrating; silly; good.)

● **How is that like the way you feel when you try to identify your gifts** or talents? (It's frustrating because I don't know what I'm good at; it's fun because I know what I do well.)

● **What did you learn about yourself during this activity?** (My talents may be more important than I had thought; I discovered something I want to do really well.)

● **How does it feel to hear other people talk about your gifts and what you can do?** (It makes me more confident; it's a little embarrassing at first.)

● **How do other people's opinions affect how you feel about yourself?** (It's great to be liked, but I usually feel pretty good about myself anyway; I get down on myself when I feel put down.)

● **How is this activity similar to what happens in real life when you try to show others who you are? How's it different?** (You only have a short time to make a good impression; people may only know a little about you; most people in real life are more critical.)

Give each person a "Talking to the Artist" handout (p. 86), a Bible, and a pencil.

Say: **Most of the time when we think about God as creator, we think about the things he created at the very beginning of time. But the Bible tells us that God never stops creating. Even as we speak, God is creating new lives and making new hearts in people. Maybe you've wondered what God is doing in your life right now. Here's an opportunity for you to talk to the artist, God, about the masterpiece he's creating in you.**

Have kids form groups of four to complete the handouts. Each person in the group can look up and read one of the Scriptures. Explain that the "you" responses are to be written privately, but the "God" responses are to be brainstormed together. Encourage kids to treat this activity as if it were really a person-to-person conversation with God.

Call groups together to discuss their responses.

Ask:

● **What was it like to "talk" to God?** (Awesome; interesting; I really couldn't get into it.)

● **What did you learn by talking to God about who you are?** (God is closer to me than I realized; God really does care about every aspect of my life.)

● **How did this "conversation" affect how you feel about yourself?** (I can see that God is working on me; I feel that God has something in mind for my life.)

● **What did you learn from this activity that will help you when you're feeling down on yourself in the future?** (I need to be patient with myself; God cares enough to keep working with me, so I must not be a total jerk.)

Say: **God will keep working on us and with us just as long as we allow him to. Choosing to put our lives in God's hands is a daily commitment.**

Talking to the Artist

Have you ever wondered what God really thinks about you? Read the following verses. Let them guide you as you fill in parts of a "conversation" between you and God.

Psalm 139:1-5

You: Is there anything about me that you don't know?

God:

Is there anything you'd like me to explain to you about yourself? If so, what?

You:

Genesis 1:27, 31

You: What does it mean to be made in your image?

God:

Why do you think I called human beings "good," even when I know how sinful they can be?

You:

Philippians 1:6; 2:13

You: What are you working on in my life right now?

God:

Isaiah 64:8

You: What kind of clay am I? Am I easy to work with, or am I a little stubborn?

God:

How do you think I would describe you as one of my creations?

You:

Mission Impossible

Purpose:

Teenagers will discover qualities of good friendships.

Supplies:

You'll need one photocopy of the "Secret Slips" handout (p. 89), scissors, nine photocopies of the "Mission Slips" handout (p. 90), newsprint, markers, and Bibles.

PointMaker

Before the meeting begins, photocopy the "Secret Slips" handout (p. 89), and cut apart the statements. Photocopy the "Mission Slips" handout (p. 90) nine times, cut out the statements, and hide these messages (along with the "Secret Slips") throughout the room.

Using your best spy impersonation, read the following directions to the students. (Wear an overcoat and hat for added effect.)

Say: **Congratulations! You've all been chosen to participate in an important and risky mission. Be careful. Here are your secret instructions: Through our informant we've learned that there are ten excellent relationship qualities out there somewhere, and we want them. If they get into the wrong hands, this mission could be a disaster. We must find them. The risk is, we've also discovered that there are many counterfeit qualities out there, so don't be fooled. These counterfeits must be found and destroyed. Therefore, for every counterfeit you turn in, you'll receive one hundred points, and for every true characteristic, the reward is fifteen hundred points. You have three minutes. Good luck!**

Have the students scour the area for the true and counterfeit qualities. When they've finished, have those who think they've found true relationship qualities come to the front, and instruct the other students to tally their points. It's OK if kids find the same qualities. Congratulate the winner, naming him or her "top spy."

Have each person who found a true quality write it on a piece of newsprint. When all ten qualities have been listed, ask:

● **How do you know these are the characteristics of a true friend, compared to the counterfeit qualities?** (They're positive things; they're things a friend should do.)

● **How was this hunt like relationships you've had?** (Good qualities are harder to find; there are a lot of false friends out there.)

● **Why wouldn't a true friend do the things on the counterfeit slips?** (They're things that destroy friendships; it would be mean.)

● **How do you feel when someone does the things listed on the newsprint?** (Special; loved; cared for; important.)

Have three teenagers volunteer to read aloud John 13:34-35; Romans 12:14-18;

and Ephesians 4:29-32.

After each volunteer reads his or her passage, have the group determine which of the ten items listed on the newsprint are mentioned. Put a check mark beside each phrase every time it's referred to. If new items are mentioned, add them to the list.

When all the verses have been read, ask:

● **What kind of friend does all these things?** (A perfect one; Jesus; a friend who loves you.)

● **Why do you think God has given us so many instructions on how to treat others?** (Because God wants our relationships to be successful; God knows we need help in friendships; God wants us to lead our friends to him.)

● **What's one friendship quality you can work on this week? How will you do this?**

Say: **If you can do the things we've listed on the newsprint, you'll certainly be the best friend anyone can find. It's not easy to be a good friend, especially when others don't treat you the same way. But God has given us specific directions for having the best relationships possible.**

Secret Slips

Love one another.

Be kind to one another.

Pray for one another.

Treat others better than yourself.

Encourage one another.

Be devoted to one another.

Forgive one another.

Respect one another.

Serve one another.

Help one another with problems.

Mission Slips

Photocopy this page nine times, and cut apart the slips so you'll have ninety slips.

Be jealous of one another.

Fight with one another.

Gossip about one another.

Trick one another.

Hate one another.

Lie to one another.

Curse one another.

Reject one another.

Be mean to one another.

Steal from one another.

Needle-Less Suffering

Purpose:
Kids will explore what the Bible says about mercy killing.

Supplies:
You'll need needles, thread, scissors, Bibles, and photocopies of the "Pros" and "Cons" lists in the margin on page 92.

PointMaker

Have kids form pairs. Give each pair two needles and a strand of thread that is at least one foot long. Say: **You'll each have a few opportunities to try to do something difficult that may cause pain or misery. Place your needles on the floor. When I say "go," pick up the needles with one hand, and put the thread through the eyes of both needles with your other hand. You must hold both needles between the finger and thumb of one hand. If you drop a needle or if one hand touches the other, you'll be disqualified.**

You'll have one minute to attempt this task. During that time, your partner must decide whether to let you continue trying to complete the task or to "put you out of your misery" by calling it quits. Your partner may not help you thread the needles. If you're put out of your misery before the time is up, you'll receive three points. If you fail to complete the task within the time limit, you won't get any points. If you successfully complete the task, you'll get fifty points.

Give each partner two attempts at the task. Then total the points for each pair, and determine the winners. Don't forget to collect the needles.

Ask:

● **Was it easy to wait and not put your partner out of his or her misery during this game? Why or why not?** (Yes, I thought my partner could thread the needles; no, I didn't think my partner could thread the needles.)

● **How is this similar to the experience of watching someone suffer from disease or physical pain?** (It's similar because you don't know how to respond; it's similar because the easy answer seems to be to put people out of their misery.)

● **What can you learn from this experience that might help you think about the practice of mercy killing (euthanasia)?** (This activity helped me see how difficult the issue is; this activity helped me see why some people might choose to let someone die rather than remain in pain.)

Say: **The issue of euthanasia is a difficult one because it involves people** who are struggling with high-powered emotions. To fully explore the impact of this kind of decision, we must look at what the Bible says about the value of life.

Have a volunteer read aloud Exodus 20:13 and Job 6:1-11. Say: **Euthanasia is the act of causing death painlessly to end suffering. Some people support euthanasia as a way to help people dying of incurable, painful diseases. Others say it's murder.**

The two Scriptures we've just read present both sides of the debate. Job wanted to die, but the Ten Commandments prohibit killing.

Ask:

● **How do these verses help us know how to respond to the issue of mercy killing?** (They don't; they only give us part of the big picture.)

Have someone read aloud Luke 10:36-37.

Ask:

● **How might someone interpret these verses in support of mercy killing?** (It's most important to do what's merciful; we should take care of terminally ill people.)

Have kids form two groups. Give a copy of the "Pros" list in the margin to one group and the "Cons" list to the other. Have groups stand facing each other, about ten feet apart. Say: **When I say "go," groups will take turns reading aloud items from their lists. As you listen to each statement, think about whether you agree or disagree with it. If you agree with the other team's statement, take one large step toward the other group. If you disagree, stay where you are. Don't follow the other group members' actions. Think about how you feel, and make your own decisions.**

Have groups alternate reading aloud one of their statements at a time.

After reading the last statement, ask kids to notice where everyone is standing.

Ask:

● **What surprised you most about the way people responded to these statements?** (We didn't all agree; we had similar responses.)

Say: **In this activity, we discovered some of the arguments for and against euthanasia. Both sides can use Scripture to support their arguments.**

At this time, present your denomination's views on euthanasia. Help kids understand why your church supports its specific beliefs. Then continue with the lesson.

Say: **One thing the Bible makes clear is that we can reach out to people who are terminally ill.**

Tell kids the names of people in your congregation or community with terminal illnesses. Then have kids pray for those people and for wisdom in knowing how to reach out to them.

Pros

1. Death would be an act of kindness for people who have incurable diseases and are in great pain.
2. Some people prefer death to a life of pain or unconsciousness.
3. Minimizing suffering is always a kind thing to do.
4. Euthanasia helps people keep their dignity; keeping them alive might make them burdens on society.
5. Euthanasia lives up to the ideal of the good Samaritan because it helps people in need.

Cons

1. God's commandment says killing is wrong.
2. Euthanasia removes the possibility of a miraculous recovery.
3. Prolonging life is always a kind thing to do.
4. Maintaining human dignity is never more important than maintaining human life.
5. The ideal of the good Samaritan means doing everything possible to maintain life while alleviating suffering.

Option Play

Purpose:

Kids will examine how their interests and personalities can help them make good career decisions.

Supplies:

You'll need shoe boxes, tape, markers, scissors, one photocopy of the "Life Points" handout (p. 95) for every two to four students, paper, pencils, and Bibles.

PointMaker

Have kids form groups of no more than four. Give each group a shoe box, tape, a marker, scissors, and a photocopy of the "Life Points" handout (p. 95). Give each person a sheet of paper and a pencil.

Have each group use its shoe box, tape, marker, and scissors to create a die (see illustration below). They'll have to cut and tape the box to make it square. Be sure kids write the numbers one through six on the die.

Tell kids they're going to play a game of Life. The object of the game is to finish with the most points: the more points gained, the more fulfilling the life. Have groups follow the rules on their "Life Points" handouts to play the game.

Have kids take turns rolling the group's die and recording the roll's point value. Whenever someone rolls a number worth more than fifty points, have group members cheer loudly. For anything worth fifty points or fewer, have group members make "buzzer" noises.

After each group plays four rounds, bring groups together, and have kids compare point totals.

Then ask:

● **What was it like to play this game?** (It wasn't fair; I was confused; I

enjoyed it because we won.)

- **How is this like the way people feel about their roles in real life? How is it different? Explain.** (It's similar because some people don't like how they live; it's different because most people get more breaks than we had in this game.)
- **How accurately do the point values reflect real life? Explain.** (Accurately—people who make more money are happier; not very accurately—just because you don't have a great job or decide not to have kids doesn't mean you can't be happy.)
- **What will it take to make you happy in the future?** (A relationship with God; a good family; a lot of money.)
- **Of all the things you could do after you graduate, what is the last thing you want to do?** (Go straight to work; live at home; join the Army; go right into college; I don't know.)

Say: **None of these things makes people better than others, but some lifestyles are more fulfilling than others. You may have a great career but work eighty hours a week. You'll quickly become overworked, exhausted, and unfulfilled. Or you may have a not-so-good job but a great family life that fulfills you. Making a good choice about what you'll do after high school isn't easy. But you can be assured that there are many good choices to be made.**

Form up to twelve groups. A group can be one person. Assign each group one or more of Jacob's sons mentioned in Genesis 49:1-28.

Give each group a Bible, a sheet of paper for each of its assigned son(s), and a pencil. Have each group read aloud Genesis 49:1-28, then create a "position wanted" ad for the son(s). Tell them to be creative, since some jobs may not be obvious. Have them include specifics about the person in each ad; for example, Reuben's ad could say, "Looking for a construction job that can use my strength. Know how to overcome any situation. Don't relate well to authority and lack self-control. Other than that, a great worker."

After groups have written their advertisements, have them read their advertisements aloud.

Then ask:

- **How difficult was it to write your ad? Explain.** (It was easy— our guy was a king; it was hard—our guy was a murderer.)
- **What connection was there between individual character qualities and work?** (Simeon and Levi were angry men, and they killed people; Joseph trusted in God, and he was a strong leader.)
- **What can you learn from this passage to help you know what your future might be?** (I can use my talents in my career; I know I can do almost anything if I really want to; there are many possibilities for my future.)

Have kids form a circle. One by one, have kids stand in the center of the circle. Have kids call out character qualities they see in the person in the center and suggest what careers he or she would be good at. Remind kids to be positive and uplifting. For example, kids may say, "Patient, a teacher"; "Kind, a doctor"; or "Helpful, a social worker."

Say: **Just as Jacob's sons each discovered a lifestyle that fit his personality, you can find a lifestyle that fits your personality.**

Life Points

Take turns rolling your homemade die and recording the point value of your roll. Play four rounds, score each round according to the list below, then total your points. The person in each group with the most points is the winner and gets the most happiness in life.

Round One

1—Physician = 100 points
2—Teacher = 75 points
3—Electrician = 75 points
4—Computer technician = 50 points
5—Waiter or Waitress = 25 points
6—Garbage collector = 10 points

Round Two

1—Married, with children = 100 points
2—Married, without children = 75 points
3—Engaged = 50 points
4—Single = 50 points
5—Divorced = 25 points
6—Widowed = 10 points

Round Three

1—$100,000 salary = 100 points
2—$60,000 salary = 75 points
3—$30,000 salary = 50 points
4—$20,000 salary = 25 points
5—Disability pension = 10 points
6—No salary = 0 points

Round Four

1—Forty-hour workweek = 100 points
2—Self-employed = 75 points
3—Business president = 75 points
4—Part-time work = 50 points
5—Eighty-hour workweek = 25 points
6—Unemployed = 10 points

Ratings Board

Purpose:

Teenagers will discover how to make wise decisions about the movies they see.

Supplies:

You'll need one photocopy of "The Ratings Game" handout (p. 99) for every two to six students, pencils, newsprint, a marker, tape, Bibles, one photocopy of the "Cecil" box (p. 97), and one photocopy of the "Elbert" box (p. 98).

PointMaker

Have kids form groups of no more than six. Say: **Imagine that your group is the ratings board for the movie industry. Your job is to evaluate movie scripts and determine what the rating of each of them should be. Today you'll each be given a handout listing films in production that need to be rated. Your job is to decide how each film should be rated and why. But before you rate the films, you'll have to determine what each rating means.**

Give each group a photocopy of "The Ratings Game" handout (p. 99) and a pencil. After a few minutes, call time. Have each group read its definitions of the five ratings. Then have groups tell how they rated each of the films. Have kids discuss why they agree or disagree with other groups' ratings.

Ask:

● **How did you feel about your group's ratings compared to everyone else's?** (They were similar; we were more conservative.)

● **What elements did you consider as you defined your ratings?** (Sexual content; violence; language; public tastes; what we liked.)

Have groups give specific examples of how they determined their ratings. For example, a group might say, "We decided G-rated films couldn't have any nudity" or "PG-13 films couldn't have more than fifteen swear words."

● **How easy was it to determine the ratings and rate each film idea? Explain.** (The ratings were tough because we didn't know where to draw the line; it was difficult to rate the films because each had good and bad aspects.)

● **How is the difficulty of rating the films like the difficulty of choosing which movies are appropriate to see?** (We each have to choose where to draw the line in what we watch; it's easy to choose what to watch.)

● **Are all films with a certain rating good or bad? Why or why not?** (No, some G-rated films are awful; no, some R-rated films have good content.)

● **What factors do you consider when you want to see a movie?** (The actors; the plot; the rating; reviews; what friends say about it.)

Say: **It would be easy to choose which movies to see if they were rated**

"OK for Christians" or "not OK for Christians." But it's not that simple. Still, we do have guidelines in the Bible to help us make those decisions. Let's take a look at those guidelines.

Ask kids to call out the names of popular current or recent movies they've seen or heard about. Tell kids the movies can have any rating. List the films on a sheet of newsprint, and tape it to the wall.

Have kids form two groups: the "Cecil" group and the "Elbert" group. Say: **In a moment we're going to have members of each group review current or recent movies from two different perspectives. The Cecil group will represent the Christian viewpoint, and the Elbert group will represent the non-Christian viewpoint.**

Give Bibles and a photocopy of the "Cecil" box in the margin to the Cecil team. Give a photocopy of the "Elbert" box (p. 98) to the Elbert group. Give groups a few minutes to discuss the strategies listed on their handouts.

Have groups sit facing each other. Randomly choose one of the films from the newsprint list. Give the Cecil and Elbert groups a moment to quickly discuss among themselves how they'll review the film. Then have each group quickly review the film aloud, based on the guidelines in the handouts. Allow each group no more than one minute to talk about what it likes or dislikes about the film and whether or not the group recommends it. Repeat this procedure for three more films (or more if time allows). If no one in either group has seen one of the movies you pick, choose another. Be sure to pick at least one R-rated film and one PG or PG-13 film.

After the reviews, have kids briefly discuss how it felt to review films from the two perspectives.

Ask:

● **What was different about the way the two groups reviewed the movies?** (The Cecil group was more concerned about the film's values; the Elbert group was more concerned about the quality of the film and the acting.)

● **What guidelines did the Scripture passages give to help the Cecil group?** (Don't go see something that might negatively affect you or another person; don't pursue things that aren't Christlike; choose wisely what to watch.)

● **How could watching a questionable movie affect another person's faith?** (The other person might begin to doubt the movie watcher's values and perhaps question his or her own as well.)

● **How can you "think only about the things in heaven, not the things on earth" in regard to watching movies?** (We can make wise decisions about the films we see; we can avoid movies altogether; we can encourage film companies to develop films with Christian viewpoints.)

Say: **Many movies today contain elements that**

Cecil

When it's your turn to review a film, use the following filters to present your views:

● Does the film encourage negative or rebellious behavior?

● Does the film contain excessive violence, nudity, evil themes, bad language, or other potentially negative elements?

● Does the film portray Christianity in a bad light?

If the movie does any of the above, it may not be worth watching.

Read the following Scripture passages and be prepared to discuss how they apply to the movies you review: Romans 14:1-10; 14:22–15:2; 2 Corinthians 6:16–7:1; Ephesians 4:17-24; and Colossians 3:1-2.

In each review, express what you like and what you don't like about the film. Then tell whether you'll recommend it, recommend it with certain cautions (explain these), or not recommend it.

Elbert

When it's your turn to review a film, use the following filters to present your views:

● Is the film well-made and well-acted?

● Does the film portray realistic characters or situations?

● Is the film entertaining?

If the movie does any of the above, it may be worth watching.

Review the films for their entertainment and artistic values, not their morality or perspectives. You believe nudity, sexual scenes, violence, and bad language may be appropriate in some movies.

In each review, express what you like and what you don't like about the film. Then tell whether you'll recommend it, recommend it with certain cautions (explain these), or not recommend it.

go against Christian principles. But if we avoid every movie with a swearword or violence, we probably won't be able to see more than a few films a year. God's guidelines can help us know where to begin, but we'll need to make intelligent decisions about the films we see. God can help us with those decisions, too.

———————————

The Ratings Game

Define each of the following ratings. Be sure to specify what elements are allowed (and how often they're allowed) for each rating.

G

PG

PG-13

R

NC-17

Now, using your ratings system, rate each of the following movies based on their script summaries:

● *Mangled Tongues of Death*—A bus load of teenagers is stranded on an abandoned toad farm, where they have to fight off a gang of escaped mental patients and their trained killer mutant toads. Contains several violent episodes (two people getting their heads chopped off), a ten-second shot of full frontal female nudity, a two-second shot of male nudity (from behind), and a lot of bad language.

Rating:

● *Bad Luck*—Two people who are forced to live on the streets because of business setbacks find each other, fall in love, and manage to escape the inner city. Contains scenes of street people eating out of trash cans, several muggings, coarse language directed at "beggars," an implied rape, depictions of prostitution and drug use, and an implied sexual relationship outside of marriage between the two main characters.

Rating:

● *Ugly People*—A science fiction thriller about a future society in which people who don't conform to public standards of attractiveness are forced to wear bags over their heads. One family decides to fight back by not wearing them. Contains realistic threats of violence, a riot scene, three instances of swearing using God's name, one scene of coarse name-calling, and a prolonged chase scene with a lot of damaged property.

Rating:

Say No

Purpose:

Kids will explore ways to combat sexual pressure.

Supplies:

You'll need two sheets of newsprint, tape, markers, Bibles, and pipe cleaners.

PointMaker

Have kids form pairs. Have guys pair up with girls as much as possible. Have partners sit in chairs facing each other. Have each pair determine which partner will be a One and which will be a Two.

Have Ones plead with Twos to switch chairs with them. Tell the Ones to beg, plead, threaten, bribe, or use any other method to convince Twos to switch.

Tell Twos not to give in to the Ones' request.

Have pairs do this for a few minutes, then have partners switch numbers and repeat the process.

Have kids form a circle, and ask:

● **How hard was it to say no?** (Not too hard; easy; difficult as time went on.)

● **How did you feel when you were pressured?** (Uncomfortable; strong.)

● **How is this situation like being pressured to have sex? How is it different?** (The pressure was strong; people tried all sorts of tactics; the arguments weren't very strong.)

● **Twos, did you ever want to give in and do what the Ones requested? Why or why not?** (Yes, I was tired of hearing him beg; no, I knew I should stand my ground.)

Tape two sheets of newsprint to the wall. Write "Tactics" on one and "How to Say No" on the other. Ask kids to name tactics the Ones used to try to convince the Twos to change seats. List these on the "Tactics" newsprint. Then have kids describe techniques Twos used to avoid giving in. List these on the "How to Say No" newsprint.

Have kids reword each "Tactic" and "How to Say No" response in terms of pressure to have sex. Discuss each of these briefly.

Then ask:

● **Which tactic listed on the newsprint is the toughest to say no to? Explain.**

● **Why do people give in and do things they don't really want to do?** (Because they're weak; they don't really know what they want; they want to make other people happy.)

Say: **Even Bible characters struggled with giving in and doing things they didn't want to do.**

Have kids form groups of no more than four. Have someone read aloud Romans 7:14-23 to the whole class.

Ask:

● **Have you ever felt the way Paul did in this passage? If so, describe that time.**

Assign one of the following passages to each group: Romans 14:1-4, 22 or Ephesians 5:1-6.

Give each group a supply of pipe cleaners. Instruct each group to sculpt a symbol that represents the message of its passage as it relates to overcoming sexual pressure. For example, a group might sculpt a person facing away from the word "sex" to illustrate Paul's advice to avoid sexual impurity. Have groups explain their sculptures to the rest of the class.

Then ask:

● **In Ephesians 5:1-6, sexual impurity is only one item among many mentioned. What can this passage, as a whole, teach us about making sexual decisions?** (We should get our lives in order and avoid temptations; we should choose only good things to think about.)

● **How might Paul's guidance in these Scriptures help you resist sexual pressure?** (It reminds me to seek God first; pressure is inevitable—I just need to work hard to avoid it.)

Say: **Like Paul, we struggle to do what God wants—and sometimes we fail. But also like Paul, we can use our knowledge and strength to help others overcome sexual pressures.**

Sell It

Purpose:
Kids will examine the powerful influence of advertising.

Supplies:
You'll need markers, paper, pencils, poster board, a prize (such as a $5 bill), Bibles, one photocopy of the "Ad Test" handout (p. 104) for each person, magazines, and food treats.

PointMaker

Have kids form teams of no more than five. Give each group markers, paper, pencils, and a sheet of poster board.

Say: **The best way to learn about advertising is to "just do it." In a few minutes, you'll each create an advertisement. The goal of your advertisement is to sell a product. You may use any approach you want with your ad, but everything you say or represent must be based on the truth.**

If another team discovers false advertising in your ad, your ad team is disqualified from the competition. The ad that best sells the product will win the team a prize of five dollars. (You may want to substitute a different prize, but money works best in this activity because it points out the main reason companies use advertisements—to make money.)

Assign each team one of the following topics (be sure at least one team has the "Christianity" topic): Christianity, Nike footwear, Pontiac cars, Pizza Hut pizza, Twinkies snack cakes, and Diet Pepsi. If you have more than six teams, assign the same product to more than one team.

Allow several minutes for teams to brainstorm and create their advertisements, using the markers and poster board. Then have teams present their advertisements and explain how they created them. Have kids vote on the best ad, without voting for their own. Award the prize to the team with the most votes.

Ask:

● **What did you notice about the approaches teams took with their ads?** (They tried to fool people; they tried to make their products sound indispensable.)

● **What did you consider as you decided how to create your ads?** (How we could get people's attention; how we could convince people they needed our product; how to fool people into thinking our product was necessary.)

● **How is that like the way advertising agencies probably think?** (They want to get people's attention; they want to make their products look great.)

● **How easy was it to sell your particular product? Explain.** (Difficult, Christianity isn't tangible like the other products; easy, everyone likes a good pizza.)

● **What elements draw people's attention to advertisements?** (Sex; humor; shocking material; strangeness.)

● **What elements shouldn't be used in advertising?** (Misleading information; sex; crudeness.)

Say: **Advertisements may try to fool us into believing something that isn't true about a product. Or they may be honest representations of the product. Whatever the method or motive behind the ad, the purpose is the same—to get us to buy the product. How should we approach advertising from a Christian perspective? Let's see what the Bible says about these issues.**

Give each student a Bible, a pencil, and an "Ad Test" handout (p. 104). Provide magazines for kids to refer to if necessary. Say: **Read the Bible passages listed on the handout, then complete the handout. When you're finished, find two other people, and discuss the questions on the handout.**

Just as kids are beginning their discussions, interrupt them with a "special offer." Bring out a food treat and say: **I've got a special deal for you today. For the low cost of giving up the rest of your discussion time, you can receive one of these fine treats.** Use descriptive words to entice kids to consider your offer. For example, you might describe how fresh and delicious the food is.

If kids "buy" the food, collect their handouts. Allow other kids to form new groups for discussion.

Allow a few more minutes for discussion, then form a circle and ask:

● **How was this activity affected by my advertisement for the food?** (No one finished the discussion; people left their groups to get food.)

● **How is this like the way advertisements can affect us in real life?** (Advertisements can affect our priorities.)

Read aloud Micah 2:6-11. Say: **These verses help us see how people tend to hear what they want to hear. Advertisers take advantage of that by presenting their products so that people "hear" only the benefits of those products.**

Ask:

● **How can we keep from being taken in by advertising?** If kids have trouble answering this question, suggest a few answers such as the following:

● Spend less time watching television.

● Investigate the product before buying it.

● Don't assume ads are telling you the whole story.

● Look "beneath" the ads to see what they're really trying to sell.

As a whole group, briefly review the discussion questions on the "Ad Test" handout.

Ad Test

Before completing this handout, read the following Scripture verses: Ephesians 5:6-8; Colossians 3:1-4; and 1 John 2:15-17.

● What guidelines do the Scripture verses give that you can apply to advertising? (An example is listed below.)

Don't focus on wanting the things advertising sells. Focus on God instead.

● Below, list five advertisements you've seen in magazines or on television. If you can't think of five, refer to one of the magazines available.

1.
2.
3.
4.
5.

● For each ad listed, describe how it tries to sell the product.

1.
2.
3.
4.
5.

● Using the guidelines from the Scriptures (and your own common sense), how should you respond to each of the advertisements you listed above?

1.
2.
3.
4.
5.

Discussion Questions:
● What would the world be like without advertising?
● What's wrong with the way companies advertise their products? What's right?
● What makes advertising successful? What makes it fail?
● How should we, as Christians, respond to advertising?
● How can we accurately "advertise" our faith?

The Stuff Race

Purpose:

Kids will examine how possessions can burden them.

Supplies:

You'll need newsprint, tape, stuffed animals, markers, and a Bible.

PointMaker

Tape a sheet of newsprint to the wall. Form two teams for a relay race. Give each team six stuffed animals and a marker.

Say: **The goal of this race is to run across the room and draw one part of a teddy bear on the newsprint, then run back and hand the marker to the next person, who will do the same. The bear parts are body, head, ears, arms, and legs. The team that draws the largest number of complete bears within four minutes is the winner.**

But there's a catch. Each runner has to carry six stuffed animals while he or she runs and draws. Ready? Let's go!

Begin the race. Listen for complaints such as "What a pain," "I can't carry all this," and "This isn't fair." When time is up and you have a winner, ask:

● **What was it like to carry all that stuff with you?** (Frustrating; it didn't bother me.)

● **When have your possessions been a burden for you?** (When I had to keep track of a camera; when I lost my wallet; when I loaned something to a friend.)

Share the comments and complaints you heard during the race.

Then read aloud Matthew 6:24, and ask:

● **How is carrying all that stuff in the race like trying to follow Jesus and holding on to a lot of possessions at the same time?** (You can't do things for God when you're busy taking care of your stuff; you can't concentrate on Jesus as well.)

Say: **We're going to run the race again. This time, though, the runner only has to carry one stuffed animal. Let's see if that makes a difference. Ready? Let's do it!**

Run the race again, but with each runner carrying only one stuffed animal. After four minutes, call time. Ask:

● **How were the two races like a relationship with Jesus?** (Getting rid of a few things can make it easier to follow him; we won't grow if we're too worried about our possessions.)

Say: **God knows our needs and promises to take care of us. He also knows we need to be free to follow him.**

The Talent Game

Purpose:

Kids will explore the importance of using their money wisely.

Supplies:

You'll need foil-wrapped candies and a Bible.

PointMaker

Distribute foil-wrapped candies to each student. To some, give ten candies. To others give five candies. And to others, give three candies. Have each person pair up with someone who has a different number of candies than he or she does. Say: **I'll make a statement about money, and you must follow the directions as stated. After each round, you may choose a new partner— but only someone who has a different number of candies. The winner will be the person with the most candy at the end. If you run out of candy during a round, don't worry—you might get some back during the next round. Keep playing until all rounds have been played.**

Read the following statements:

Round 1
- **Take one piece of candy from your partner if you presently receive an income of any kind.**
- **Take one piece of candy from your partner if you put some of your income in a savings account.**
- **Take one piece of candy from your partner if you can identify how every penny of your last payment was used.**

Round 2
- **Take one piece of candy from your partner if you spend less than half of your present income on personal pleasure.**
- **Take one piece of candy from your partner if you've never wagered and lost a bet.**
- **Take one piece of candy from your partner if you've ever read a book or article on personal finances.**

Round 3
- **Take two pieces of candy from your partner if you have a job that allows time off for church and youth meetings.**
- **Take two pieces of candy from your partner if you can cite (within two cents) the present price of regular unleaded gasoline.**
- **Take two pieces of candy from your partner if you've recently used a coupon to buy a product at a grocery store.**

Round 4

● Take two pieces of candy from your partner if you have a savings account of any kind.

● Take two pieces of candy from your partner if you've never spent more fixing something (such as a bicycle or car) than it was worth.

● Take two pieces of candy from your partner if you've personally given money to a church offering.

Round 5

● Take three pieces of candy from your partner if you presently give 10 percent of your income to the church.

● Take three pieces of candy from your partner if you've never spent more than five dollars on any one "impulse" purchase.

● Take three pieces of candy from your partner if you've developed a personal spending budget.

● Take three pieces of candy from your partner if you've bought something worth more than eight hundred dollars and paid it off.

Have the group come back together and count the pieces of candy to determine the winner.

Ask:

● **What were your thoughts when some people received more pieces of candy than you did?** (I felt hurt; I wondered why; I questioned my ability to play the game.)

● **How is this like the way wealth is spread out in real life?** (Some people have more money than others; some people don't start with much.)

● **What actions brought you more pieces of candy?** (Proper money management; savings; giving to church.)

● **Were you satisfied with your final candy count? Why or why not?** (No, I wanted more; yes, I had plenty.)

Say: **Developing good spending habits can help you use your money wisely. Think about how well you did in this game. If you didn't take many pieces of candy from your partner, ask yourself why.**

Have kids name examples of poor money management. Then have kids call out examples of good money management.

Have someone read aloud Matthew 25:14-30.

Ask:

● **What does this story tell us about money?** (You need to invest wisely; you need to take care of your money; it's OK to make money.)

Say: **The parable of the talents isn't just about money. It's also about being responsible with what God has entrusted to us. And if we simply toss our money away on things that may make us happy for a moment, we aren't being good stewards. The best way to begin developing good stewardship and money-management habits is by developing a budget to help us control our spending.**

Have kids share ideas about how they can begin using budgets, then ask group members to make a commitment to create and follow budgets for a month. Plan to follow up on this activity within a month to discuss what kids learned from the experience.

This Is Your Life, Life, Life...

Purpose:

Kids will discover the difference between reincarnation and resurrection.

Supplies:

You'll need white and black beads, a paper bag, and a Bible.

PointMaker

Put some beads in a paper bag, one-fourth white beads and three-fourths black beads. (You could use black and white jelly beans or black and white squares of paper instead of beads.) Place the bag at the front of the room.

Say: **Eventually everyone dies. And because death is inevitable, people are curious about it. People wonder what happens after death. One belief is that people are reincarnated, but the Bible doesn't teach us about reincarnation; it teaches us the truth—about resurrection. Though these concepts may sound somewhat similar, reincarnation is very different from resurrection. Let's find out what reincarnation is.**

Tell kids to imagine that instead of being given one life to live, they have to live as many lives as it takes to become perfect.

Have everyone form a line and walk past the bag. As they pass, have them each take five beads without looking. Tell kids who have all white beads that they're "perfect" and may sit down. Have the other kids go through the line again, drop their previously chosen beads back into the bag, and pick five new beads.

Have kids continue to go through the line as many as five times. Few of them will have picked five white beads.

Ask:

● **How easy was it to collect five white beads? Explain.** (Very easy, I picked them on the first try; difficult, I always had at least one black bead.)

● **How much control did you have in getting the beads you wanted?** (None—it was all luck.)

Say: **The theory of reincarnation is a lot like this game. In reincarnation, people must be reborn again and again in their quest to finally become perfect. How well people do in a particular "life" determines their advantages as they start the next "round." Some people who believe in reincarnation feel bound by the actions of past lives—with little hope of escape.**

Ask:

● **What was it like to try to get five white beads?** (Frustrating; it wasn't easy; I was hopeful.)

Say: **Reincarnation is a popular belief among New Agers and people who practice Eastern religions such as Hinduism. But the Bible teaches us about a different kind of rebirth.**

Have someone read aloud John 11:23-25.

Give each person a white bead. Say: **When Jesus died for our sins, he gave us the promise of resurrection. There's no "cosmic lottery" system to determine whether you'll end up with five white beads someday. God's promise is both simple and powerful: Someday, when Christ returns, believers in Christ will be given new heavenly bodies and we'll live eternally with Jesus. Just as you were each given one white bead as a gift, so resurrection is given to each of us as a gift from God.**

This Little Light of Mine

Purpose:
Kids will discover how each person can make a big difference in his or her school.

Supplies:
You'll need a room that can be darkened, small candles, matches, and a Bible.

PointMaker

Have students stand in a circle. Give everyone a small, unlit candle, then turn off any lights in the room.

Ask:

● **How is this darkened room like your school?** (Some people are lost in the darkness; sometimes kids can't see the way to go.)

● **Being a student involves a lot of different things—what are some ways you can be a light for God in your activities at school?** (I can speak kind words; encourage others; reach out to lonely kids.)

Say: **We're going to light one another's candles to brighten this room. As you light the candle of the person next to you, name one way you view that person as a light for God.**

Light your candle, and use it to light the candle of the student on your right while sharing an affirming statement with that person. Then have that person light the candle of the person to his or her right and share an affirming statement. (If you have a large group, light the candles of the students on both sides of you so the flame and affirmations will move faster.)

Ask:

● **How has the room changed now that all these candles are lit?** (We can see each other's faces; it's much brighter.)

● **How is the way each small candle helped to brighten the room like the way you can each brighten your school?** (If each person here makes a small difference, the cumulative difference will be great; people will notice the little things we do.)

Read aloud Matthew 5:14-16.

Say: **A bunch of small lights can quickly brighten up a dark place. Being a student gives you the potential to be a light for God and to brighten your school.**

Have kids blow out their candles.

Time-Travel Troubles

Purpose:
Kids will explore ways to develop Christlike friendships.

Supplies:
You'll need paper, pencils, one photocopy of the "Interests" handout (p. 113) for each person, and a Bible.

PointMaker

Have kids form pairs. Give each pair a sheet of paper that has a different activity written on it. Use these ideas, or come up with your own:
- starting a car
- plugging in and turning on a lamp
- making a phone call
- typing the alphabet on a typewriter
- making a glass of lemonade with ice in it
- riding a bicycle

Explain that you are a cave dweller who has just been transported from millions of years ago to the present through a strange accident. Say: **In order to get by, I'm going to have to learn how to do some things. Each pair has a paper with an activity written on it. I need partners to explain to me exactly how to do their activity.**

Give each pair one or two minutes to explain the activity. Make the activity as difficult as possible for them to explain. For example, if they say, "Get in the car," ask, "What's a car?" For every answer they give, ask another question.

After partners have made a brief attempt at their explanations, ask all the students:
- **How did you feel when you were trying to explain a simple activity to the cave dweller?** (Frustrated; I thought it was funny.)
- **How was this activity like trying to talk to a member of the opposite sex?** (Guys are cave men; girls ask too many questions; you can't figure out where they're coming from.)
- **What are some differences in the ways guys and girls communicate?** (Girls talk too much; guys brag a lot.)

Say: **Sometimes talking to members of the opposite sex is like talking to people from a different time period. It seems that they don't understand us and we don't understand them. But if we don't communicate,** things never work out and both sides become frustrated and confused. One way we can communicate better and build friendships with others is to learn more about them.

Give each person an "Interests" handout (p. 113) and a pencil. Give kids three minutes to fill out as much of the handout as possible. Encourage kids to get as many names as possible on their surveys.

After three minutes, gather the group together, and see who was able to complete the survey.

Read aloud Philippians 2:3-8. Ask:

● **How do these verses apply to the way we should relate to others?** (We should be interested in other people, not ourselves; we should put others first.)

● **How do these verses apply to guy—girl relationships?** (You need to put the other person first; you have to genuinely care about the other person.)

● **How do you feel when someone you go out with agrees to do something you enjoy, even though you know it's not his or her favorite activity?** (It makes me feel special; I believe she's really interested in me.)

Say: **It was hard to communicate with the cave dweller because you didn't have much in common. Now we have found a few things that we have in common, and we know it's important to put others' interests before our own. We can do this by doing more listening and less talking and by sincerely showing an interest in our friends' lives.**

———————————————

Interests

See if you can find out new things about people in our group. Find the following people, and have them each initial the appropriate space.

A girl who likes football and knows what a safety is: ____

A person who likes to eat at McDonald's: ____

Someone who doesn't like chocolate: ____

A guy who likes to make and eat brownies: ____

A girl who likes to sing in the shower: ____

Someone who likes classical music: ____

A person who has been on a mission trip or wants to go on one: ____

Someone who likes the same kind of music you do: ____

A person who doesn't like pizza: ____

A guy who likes to go to the movies: ____

A person who does volunteer work in our community: ____

A girl who is on a sports team: ____

Someone who recycles aluminum cans or newspapers: ____

Someone who sings in a choir: ____

A person who likes to try new foods: ____

Someone who enjoys math: ____

Someone who has a hobby in common with you: ____

A girl who is terrible at bowling but likes to go bowling anyway: ____

A guy who likes to visit museums: ____

Tower Races

Purpose:

Kids will explore how God's definition of success compares with the world's.

Supplies:

You'll need paper cups, newsprint, markers, tape, pencils, a photocopy of the "What, Me Worry?" handout (p. 116) for each person, and Bibles.

PointMaker

Have kids form teams of no more than four. Have each team find a space in the room away from the other teams. Give each team at least thirty paper cups (or you can use children's blocks or plastic foam cups). On "go," have teams compete to build the best free-standing tower in two minutes.

After two minutes, call time.

Ask:

● **How easy was it to build a tower in two minutes? Explain.** (Not very easy, two minutes isn't much time; easy, we just worked quickly.)

● **Which aspect of the tower did you focus on more: its sturdiness or its height? Explain.** (Its height, because a taller tower would look better; it's sturdiness, because a weak foundation wouldn't allow much height in the tower.)

Say: **Building a tower in two minutes can be like trying to build a successful life on earth according to society's definition of success. What we think is the best or tallest is still dwarfed by God's kingdom. What we think has a solid foundation is easily toppled.**

Have kids see how much jostling their towers can stand before they fall. Then say: **People don't like to think that their wealth or possessions will someday be gone. But just as your towers didn't last forever, neither will money or riches.**

Have kids brainstorm several reasons people desire wealth today—to achieve security, fame, or greed, for example. Write these reasons on a sheet of newsprint, and tape it to the wall.

Then give each person a "What, Me Worry?" handout (p. 116) and a pencil. Read aloud Luke 12:13-34, then have students follow the instructions on the handout. Help coordinate the activities as necessary, then have kids form groups of no more than five to discuss the questions at the bottom of the handout. Encourage students to talk about how they felt as they followed the handout's instructions.

Have kids form a circle, then ask:

● **If Jesus were to write a book today, what would he tell us about riches and wealth?** (Don't worry about money; money can be dangerous; money is only temporary.)

● **Define success in God's eyes as opposed to the world's eyes.** (Giving instead of getting; being humble instead of boasting; serving others instead of demanding to be served.)

Say: **The world's view of success is measured in dollars and cents. But God's view of success is measured by our faith in him.**

Have volunteers share ideas of ways to serve God in everyday activities. Then close in a group prayer, asking God to help each group member discover the true meaning of success through increasing their faith.

———————————————————

What, Me Worry?

After listening to Luke 12:13-34, follow the instructions on this handout. In a few minutes you'll join a group to discuss the questions at the bottom of the page.

● The Scripture passage describes some of life's worries. Talk with at least two other people about one of the worries the passage describes.

● You may have worries similar to those addressed in the Scripture passage. Find a partner, and take turns pantomiming your worries for each other. See how quickly your partner can guess your worry. If you can't think of any worries, consider these: not having enough money, not getting a job, getting sick, becoming a victim of violence.

● Read the Scripture passage. Then ask other people to help you find Jesus' answers to the worries of life in each verse listed below. Write your answers in the space provided.

Verse 23   Life is more than food.

Verse 24

Verse 27

Verse 28

Verse 29

Verse 31

Verse 33

● Think of a popular song that expresses your worries about life. Sing the first line of that song for someone else, or simply tell someone the title of the song.

Discussion Questions
● How do each of Jesus' answers about life's worries apply today?

● What do these verses tell us about society's fascination with wealth?

● Do these verses say money isn't important? Why or why not?

● What is your personal response to these verses? Explain.

Troublemaker

Purpose:
Kids will explore the pressures they feel at home.

Supplies:
You'll need one photocopy of the "Troublemaker" handout (p. 119) for every five students, scissors, bowls, a bag of small candies, newsprint, markers, Bibles, and tape.

PointMaker

Photocopy the "Troublemaker" handout (p. 119) once for every five students. Cut the handout as indicated, and place each set of strips in a bowl or another small container. Have kids form groups of no more than five. Give each group a set of "Troublemaker" strips, and have each person draw a strip and secretly read it.

Hint
If a group has less than five members, have students draw strips until all the strips have been taken. Students with two strips should follow the instructions on both strips.

Say: **Someone in your group is a troublemaker, and you've got to find out who it is. Follow the instructions on the strip you drew, and don't let anyone else see your strip. You have five minutes to determine who the troublemaker is. If your group correctly names the troublemaker, everyone but the troublemaker will share this prize.** Show the bag of candy. **If your group names the wrong troublemaker, the real troublemaker will get the prize.**

Allow five minutes for discussion, then have each group guess the identity of its troublemaker. Award prizes to groups guessing correctly or to troublemakers whose groups guessed incorrectly.

Ask:

● **How did you decide who the troublemaker was?** (We picked the most negative person in our group; everyone was making trouble, so we couldn't choose just one person.)

● **How did you feel during the discussion? Explain.** (Frustrated because everyone was so crabby; guilty for picking on everyone; glad everyone was focusing on someone else instead of me.)

● **What kind of pressure did you feel?** (Pressure to blame someone else; pressure to win the prize; pressure to stop the arguing.)

● **How was this discussion like life in your home?** (My family's always arguing; everyone's always blaming someone else instead of working on the problems; every family has problems; even small problems cause tension.)

● **What kinds of pressures do you feel at home?** (Pressure to live up to my mom's expectations; pressure to get good grades; pressure to solve my family's problems; pressure to earn money.)

Have volunteers write out these Bible passages on sheets of newsprint: Psalm 17:6-8; Ephesians 4:32; Ephesians 6:1-3; and Colossians 3:12-14. Tape one passage in each corner of the room.

Have everyone read the verses aloud in unison.

Say: **I'm going to describe a variety of situations. Choose one Bible passage from those in the four corners that you think offers guidance for the situation. Stand in the corner where that passage is displayed.**

Read the following situations, and have students move to the corners they've chosen. Then ask the indicated question and have students from each represented corner respond.

Situation one: **Your parents don't approve of the person you're dating.**

After students have chosen passages and moved to the appropriate corners, ask:

● **How does this passage apply to this situation?** (It tells me to obey my parents; it tells me to forgive my parents even though I think they're wrong.)

Situation two: **Your parents expect too much of you. Your grades are always expected to be A's; and you have to be the best in sports, earn your own spending money, and be active at church. You're running out of time and energy!**

After students have chosen passages and moved to the appropriate corners, ask:

● **Based on the message of your passage, what could you do in this situation?** (Talk to God; calmly talk to my parents; express my feelings in a loving way.)

Situation three: **Your mom lost her job, and you're scared about the future.**

After students have chosen passages and moved to the appropriate corners, ask:

● **How can this passage help you cope in this situation?** (God will take care of me; I need to show love to my mom; we can make it if we pull together.)

Situation four: **Your sister is driving you crazy. She gets into your stuff, is rude, and always embarrasses you in front of your friends. You can't stand being near her anymore!**

After students have chosen passages and moved to the appropriate corners, ask:

● **Using your passage as a guideline, how should you act in this situation?** (I should show love to my sister; be patient and forgiving toward her; be an example to her of love and kindness.)

Have students return to their seats. Ask:

● **According to the Bible, what's your responsibility in your home?** (To be kind; to trust God; to be patient; to obey my parents; to avoid starting fights.)

● **How will doing these things relieve pressure?** (It prevents fights; knowing God's in control prevents me from feeling stressed.)

Say: **No matter how bad the pressure is at home, God is with us and can give us strength and guidance.**

Troublemaker

Photocopy this page, and cut the following instructions into strips. You'll need one set for every five students.

You're the troublemaker, but don't admit it. Place the blame on another person.

Complain about what slobs your group members are. They're *all* troublemakers as far as you're concerned.

Accuse the person on your right. Be as loud and obnoxious as possible.

Threaten to leave the group if others don't agree with your opinion. Be sure everyone hears what you have to say.

Keep telling everyone how perfect you are. You'd never cause problems because you're so good.

Weighty Choices

Purpose:

Kids will examine the temptation to explore sex.

Supplies:

You'll need sealable plastic bags, water, paper bags, a scale, paper, a pencil, and Bibles.

PointMaker

Place varying amounts of water in at least ten sealable plastic bags. Make sure the partially empty bags are inflated with air so they'll take up the same amount of space as those filled with water.

Place each plastic bag in a separate paper bag so kids can't tell how much the paper bags weigh by looking at them. Line up the bags on a table. Have a scale available that can measure as little as two pounds.

Show teenagers the bags and the scale. Say: **In a moment you'll compete to see who can identify how many bags it takes to reach a total weight of two pounds. The person whose guess is closest to two pounds, without going over, will win.**

Here's how it works: When it's your turn to guess, you must choose which bags you'll place on the scale. Once you touch a bag, you must use it. You may place the bags on the scale only after you've chosen all the bags you're going to use.

Beginning with the person who got up the earliest this morning, have kids take turns choosing bags and placing them on the scale. Warn kids not to be too rough with the bags. As kids choose which bags they want, encourage them to keep taking "just one more."

Put the bags back on the table after each person is finished, and have kids look away while you shuffle them around. On a sheet of paper, record the total weight of each person's selections. Have kids give a round of applause to the person whose choices come closest to two pounds without going over.

Then ask:

● **What was going through your mind as you participated in this activity?** (I wanted to win; I was worried that I'd choose too many bags.)

● **How is the temptation to take "one more bag" like the temptation to explore sexual feelings in a relationship?** (You try to go as far as possible without doing something you'll regret later; it's easy to believe you're doing the right thing.)

● **How is the way I encouraged you to take more bags like the pressures kids feel to have sex?** (Our friends all say it's unnatural to be a virgin; the media says it's right to have sex when you want to.)

Say: **When two people begin serious dating, they become closer in** many ways, and the pressure to give in to sexual desires becomes stronger and stronger. Unfortunately, dealing with these desires isn't always easy.

Have volunteers read aloud 2 Samuel 11:2-5, 12-15.

Ask:

● **What were the consequences of David's decision?**

● **How did those consequences affect others?**

Then say: **When we make choices, we must be ready for the consequences. But the consequences don't affect only the people making the decisions. David may have been ready to deal with the choices he made, but what about Uriah, who eventually died because of David's choices? Part of making good decisions about dating and sex is realizing that your actions affect other people.**

Who Wants a Penny?

Purpose:

Kids will learn that leadership qualities must be cultivated in order to grow.

Supplies:

You'll need a calculator and Bibles.

PointMaker

Say: **Let's say you have an opportunity to receive either one million dollars in cash or one penny. If the total amount of the penny doubled every year and was added to the existing total each year for the next twenty years, which would you choose: the million dollars or the penny?**

Now show your class what those who chose the penny would actually receive. The formula is simple: Multiply .01 x 3, and multiply that total x 3, and multiply that total x 3, and so on, once for each year through twenty.

Have someone ready with a calculator to help you demonstrate that at the end of year one, those who chose the penny would have three pennies. At the end of year two, they would have nine pennies. At the end of year three, they would have twenty-seven pennies, and so on. After twenty years, the grand total would be $34,867,844.01.

Ask:

● **Does it seem possible that one little penny could turn into so much money? Why or why not?** (No, I'm still not sure what you did; yes, I remember doing this in my math class.)

Say: **There is a life principle in this activity. Small things, if cultivated, can grow into big things. As you think about leadership, you might not feel that you have much of an opportunity to be a leader right now. But if you'll be patient and faithful with small opportunities, bigger ones await you.**

Form three groups, and assign each group one of these passages: 1 Samuel 16:1-13; Matthew 25:14-30; or 1 Timothy 4:12. After reading its passage, have each group create a human sculpture that represents the message of the passage.

When groups are ready, have them present their sculptures and explain them. Applaud groups' efforts.

Ask each group:

● What does your passage teach us about developing our leadership skills right now?

Say: **Great leaders don't start out being great. They start small, with seemingly insignificant responsibilities. To become leaders, we must learn to be responsible with the small opportunities we have right now.**

Scripture Index

Topic Index

Group Publishing, Inc.
Attention: Books & Curriculum
P.O. Box 481
Loveland, CO 80539
Fax: (970) 669-1994

Evaluation for POINTMAKER™ DEVOTIONS FOR YOUTH MINISTRY

Please help Group Publishing, Inc., continue to provide innovative and useful resources for ministry. Please take a moment to fill out this evaluation and mail or fax it to us. Thanks!

● ● ●

1. As a whole, this book has been (circle one)

not very helpful   very helpful

1   2   3   4   5   6   7   8   9   10

2. The best things about this book:

3. Ways this book could be improved:

4. Things I will change because of this book:

5. Other books I'd like to see Group publish in the future:

6. Would you be interested in field-testing future Group products and giving us your feedback? If so, please fill in the information below:

Name _____

Street Address _____

City _____ State _____ Zip _____

Phone Number _____ Date _____